Passive Income With Dividend Investing

Your

Step-By-Step Guide To

Make **Money In The** Stock Market

Using Dividend Stocks

By

Michael Ezeanaka

www.MichaelEzeanaka.com

Copyright ©2019

Disclaimer

This publication is designed to provide competent and reliable information regarding the subject matter covered. However, it is sold with the understanding that the author is not engaged in rendering investment or other professional advice. Laws and practices often vary from state to state and country to country and if investment or other expert assistance is required, the services of a professional should be sought. The author specifically disclaims any liability that is incurred from the use or application of the contents of this book.

Books In The Business and Money Series	
Series #	**Book Title**
1	Affiliate Marketing
2	Passive Income Ideas
3	Affiliate Marketing + Passive Income Ideas (2-in-1 Bundle)
4	Facebook Advertising
5	Dropshipping
6	Dropshipping + Facebook Advertising (2-in-1 Bundle)
7	Real Estate Investing For Beginners
8	Credit Cards and Credit Repair Secrets
9	Real Estate Investing And Credit Repair (2-in-1 Bundle)
10	Passive Income With Affiliate Marketing (2nd Edition)
The kindle edition will be available to you for FREE when you purchase the paperback version from Amazon.com (The US Store)	

Download The Audio Versions Along With The Complementary PDF Document For FREE from **www.MichaelEzeanaka.com/My Audiobooks**

Table of Contents

Thousands of people in the US have their own business, earning profits regularly, without even showing up at work. For many of us, it is an ideal life - relaxing, watching the business grow, and receiving money from dividend payouts.

This is possible if you own an investment portfolio composed of stocks. Not only mere stocks but company stocks that will allow you to earn passive income.
In our attempt to build wealth, we have invented stocks, which is now considered as one of the best financial instruments in the world.

Savvy investors have a significant percentage of their investment in stocks. In your quest towards financial freedom, you have to understand the nature of stocks, and how you can be successful investing in dividends.

Through the years, more and more people are becoming more interested in the stock market. While in the past, this platform was often reserved for members of the high society, at present, the stock market is now accessible to many and it's indeed a popular instrument for growing private wealth.

This popularity alongside considerable technological advances used in stock trading has liberated the stock market so that anyone can reap its rewards and have the chance to succeed in growing their investments.

But despite the popularity, many are still not fully aware of the benefits and drawbacks of dividend investing. Unfortunately, much information about dividend stocks revolve around conversations over the water cooler with people who are not fully knowledgeable of the financial instrument.

Chances are, you have already heard your friends saying things like "Never trust the stock market. It is only for the rich. You will just lose your money in seconds!" or "My cousin made thousands of dollars with ABC Inc, so I am also investing my savings..."

Much of this misinformation is largely based on the mindset of overnight success, which was specifically popular during the dotcom bubble of the 90s. Unfortunately, people still think that stocks will help them get rich quick without much effort or proper risk assessment.

This sad fact was confirmed when the dotcom bubble popped. It is true that stocks can make you rich, and if you invest in dividend stocks, it will allow you to earn passive income. However, at all times, you should be aware of the risks you are exposed to.

The best way to combat ignorance is through education. The key to making sure that you will be profitable in dividend investing is to **know where you are investing your money.**

This is the reason why I decided to write this book - to educate you on the fundamentals of dividend investing. This book will help you understand:

- The advantages and disadvantages of investing in dividend stocks
- Key technical terms that you will surely encounter while you explore the world of dividend investing
- Different factors that you need to consider when investing in dividend stocks
- Different strategies you can employ when investing in dividends including high dividend yield strategy and high dividend growth rate strategy (The two major schools of thought when it pertains to dividend investing)

And a whole lot more!

The investment principles discussed in this book are not new. I believe there is no need to reinvent the wheel. There are hundreds of investment experts who are already using and advocating the strategies that you will learn here. But I think I have presented these things in a way that an average investor can easily understand.

In the final chapter of this book, a case study will be presented. This case study puts together all the concepts discussed in previous chapters and shows you how a typical dividend investor makes decisions starting from stock purchase to eventual sale – this will help you consolidate your understanding and gain confidence in your ability to invest wisely.

Are you excited yet? Let's get right into it!

Interesting Fact #1

There are few things that income-seeking investors like more than buying into companies that have paid a dividend for decades or longer. The reason is that a steady history of payouts often establishes to investors the health of a business model. Only a handful of currently traded companies have paid out dividends for longer than 100 years, and I can find no company that has paid dividends in a concurrent manner for longer than the **Bank of Montreal** (NYSE:BMO), which has been divvying out dividend payments since 1829!

Chapter 1

Why Invest In Dividend Stocks

Investing in dividend stocks can be right for you if you are looking for an investment that provides regular income. Dividend-paying companies regularly distribute a percentage of their profits to investors. Moreover, many dividend stocks in the US are paying investors a fixed amount every quarter, while there are other companies that increase their payouts over time. Hence, it's not unreasonable to expect (after building your portfolio of dividend stocks) a cash stream that resembles an annuity.

Why Some Companies Pay Dividends, While Others Don't

There are several reasons why a company may choose to pass some of its profits as dividends, and another set of reasons why some companies prefer not to issue dividends and instead use all the earnings for growth.

For a stable company with regular earnings that doesn't require reinvestments, dividend payouts can be a good idea because:

- Many investors see dividend payouts as an indicator that the company is strong. It is also a sign that the company has positive projections for earnings in the future that makes the stock more enticing. Remember, higher demand for a company stock will boost its price
- Many investors are looking for steady income that is linked with dividends so they will be more likely to purchase the company's stocks.

US companies that are paying dividends include Verizon (VZ), Wells Fargo (WFC), Exxon Mobil (XOM), Microsoft (MSFT), and Apple (AAPL).

On the other hand, some companies choose not to issue dividends because of the following reasons:

- Startup companies that are rapidly growing will not issue dividends because it needs to invest as much as possible into their growth
- Established companies also choose not to issue dividends if its directors believe it will do a better job of increasing its share price through reinvestment.
- Some companies choose to temporarily suspend dividends to begin a new project, buy out another company, or repurchase some of their shares.
- Companies that choose to reinvest all their profits, rather than issuing dividends may also think about the expensive cost of new stock issuance. To stay away from raising funds through this channel, they decide to keep the profits.
- The decision to begin paying dividends or to increase a current dividend rate is a huge business decision. Firms that will suddenly cancel or even reduce its current dividend payout could be viewed unfavorably and the share price may decrease as a result.

US companies that historically decided not to pay dividends include Tesla, Biogen, Amazon, Alphabet, and Facebook.

Types of Dividends

Basically, a dividend is a cash payout issued by shareholders of a company. But there are different types of dividends, some of which don't involve the payment of cash to stockholders. Below are the different types of dividends:

1. Cash Dividend

Most dividends are considered as cash dividends in form of electronic transfer or check. The value of the cash dividend will be transferred from the company to the stockholders instead of the former using this percentage of the profit for its growth or operations.

If a company decides to issue a cash dividend that is equivalent to the 5 percent of the share price, you can see a resulting loss of 5 percent in the share price. This is caused by the economic value transfer.

Another effect of cash dividends is that the recipients of cash dividends should pay tax on the distribution value, which can lower down its final value.

However, cash dividends can be beneficial for the investors because it will provide you with regular passive income on your investment on top of the possible appreciation of your capital investment.

2. Stock Dividend

Stock dividends are issued by a company to its shareholders without consideration. Most stock dividends are common stocks. When a company issues less than 25% of the total number of outstanding shares, then the transaction is considered as stock dividends. On the other hand, the transaction is considered a stock split if the transaction is in a higher proportion of the outstanding shares.

If a company decides to issue a 5 percent stock dividend, it should increase the number of shares by 5 percent. If you are a stockholder of this company, you will be entitled with 1 share for every 20 shares you own. If you have 1 million shares in the company, you will gain 50,000 additional shares.

However, this doesn't increase the company's value. If the share price of a company is at $10/share, then the value of the company will be at $10 million. After the issuance of the stock dividend, the company's value shall remain the same, but the price will be lower at $9.50 because of the settlement of the stock dividend.

One primary advantage of a stock dividend is you will have a choice. You may either retain your shares and bet that the company will use the cash to increase its share price or you may choose to sell some of your shares so you can convert your stocks into cash.

Cash Dividend Vs. Stock Dividend

Cash dividend seems a better choice if you want an automatic reward for placing your investments in certain companies. But this is not always true.

In various ways, it is better for both the shareholder and the company to choose stock dividends at least once a year. A stock dividend is also good as cash with the extra advantage of not paying taxes upon receipt.

You are a multi-millionaire today if you are one of the early investors who purchased Microsoft's shares in 1986. At least 100 shares of this stock at $21 per share now increased to 28,000 shares. This was the reason why Bill Gates became the richest man in the world.

One of the main reasons for issuing stock dividends instead of cash dividends could be that in doing so, a company and its stockholders can establish stronger links with investors acquiring more of the company with the extra shares.

As long as they are not bundled with a cash option, stock dividends are considered superior to cash dividends. Companies that are paying stock dividends are providing their stockholders the option to convert the shares into cash or keep their profit.

There is no other option if you choose the cash dividend.

However, this doesn't mean that cash dividends are not good. The only downside of this dividend is the limit in your options. You can still choose to reinvest your cash dividends into the company via a reinvestment plan.

Meanwhile, choosing stock dividends is not always a better alternative than taking the cash. Remember, the stock market is very unpredictable. The value of shares could drastically be affected by economic turmoils such as the Great Depression of 1929 and the Global Financial Recession of 2008.

3. Liquidating Dividend

Liquidating dividend are issued when the board of directors of a company decides to return the capital originally paid by stockholders as a dividend. This usually a bad indicator because this dividend is often paid before the business shuts down.

Companies issuing liquidating dividends may choose to pay the bill in one or several installments. US companies are mandated to issue Form 1099-DIV to all its stockholders that contain all the information about the payout.

Even with several tax benefits, liquidating dividends may not be enough to cover initial investment as the fundamental quality of the company may have significantly plummeted.

4. Scrip Dividend

Scrip dividends are issued by companies who don't have enough funds to issue dividends anytime soon.

This type of dividend is basically a promissory note to pay stockholders at a certain date.
The promissory note creates a note payable and may or may not include interest

5. Property Dividend

Companies may choose to issue the non-monetary dividend as an alternative to stock or cash payment. This type of property dividend may either include shares of a subsidiary organization or any physical assets that are owned by the company like real estate, equipment, or inventories.

Property dividends are recorded at the market value of the asset distributed. Investors may choose to hold the asset for possible capital gains, but this is usually for the long-term perspective especially with real estate dividends.

This form of payout scheme is less common compared to cash or stock dividend system. From a corporate perspective, property dividends could be distributed if the main company doesn't have sufficient cash on hand to distribute significant payouts or it doesn't want to dilute its existing share position.

Even though these are considered non-cash dividends, property dividends still have cash value.

How Do Companies Pay Dividends

Companies usually pay dividends in form of a check, but some also issue dividends as stock options.
The normal process for dividend payment is a check that is often sent to shareholders a few days after the former dividend date, the date on which the stock begins trading without the declared dividend.

On the other hand, some companies issue additional shares equivalent to the amount of dividend payout. This alternative is known as dividend reinvestment and often provided as a dividend payment option by mutual funds and individual companies.

Take note that dividends are taxable income regardless of the form you received them.

Dividend Reinvestment Plans or DRIPs provide several benefits to investors. If you want to simply add your present equity holdings with any added funds from dividend payments, a plan can simplify the process as opposed to getting the dividend payment in monetary form and then using the money to buy more shares.

In-house reinvestment plans are often commission-free because you don't need to pay brokerage fees. This attribute makes it enticing for small investors because commission fees are proportionately bigger for smaller stock purchases.

Another advantage of a reinvestment plan is that some companies are offering shareholders the opportunity to buy added shares in cash at a lower price.

The price reduction can go between 1 and 10% on top of the additional benefit of waived broker fees. So you can buy more stock holdings at a discounted price over investors who buy shares in cash through brokerage fees.

When to Expect Dividend Payout

If a company decides to issue dividends, stockholders are notified through a press release, and the news will also be reported via major stock quoting services for easier reference.

Upon announcement, a schedule will be set or a record date, which means all stockholders on this date will be entitled to the payout. The day after the record date is known as ex-date, which refers to the date that the stock starts trading ex-dividend.

Hence, if you acquire shares on an ex-date, you will not be eligible for the payout. Usually, the payable date is 30 days after the record date.

When the payable date arrives, the company will deposit the dividends with the Depository Trust Company (DTC). Payouts are then distributed by the DTC to brokerage companies around the globe where stockholders are holding the shares of the company.

In turn, the brokerage firms will deposit cash payouts to their client accounts or process reinvestment plans upon the instruction of the shareholder.

Preferred Stocks Vs. Common Stocks

Preferred stockholders are usually prioritized when it comes to claiming the company's earnings and assets. This covers the issuance of dividends, wherein preferred shareholders are paid before common stockholders.

Advantages of Dividend Investing

Somehow, receiving dividends is like getting interest on your bank savings. It can be quite nice but doesn't provide the thrill from betting on the rise and fall of share prices. People love the exhilarating experience especially when prices are soaring. However, if you are a conservative investor, dividend stocks provide several benefits over investing on non-dividend stocks.

Below are some of the reasons why it is beneficial for investors to choose dividend stocks:

1. Passive Income

Dividends from stocks can provide you a regular flow of passive income than you may choose to reinvest or spend. This is the main attribute that attracts many retirees who are looking for supplemental income.

2. Lower Risk

Dividend stocks have less volatility in share price and they usually have a lower risk-to-reward ratio. Because of these attributes, dividend stocks can experience a minimal decline in the share price during a market downturn. Lower volatility can also temper the appreciation of the share price during market recovery.

3. More Stable Companies

Dividend stocks are often paid by companies that are more stable. Startup companies usually don't pay dividends as they need to reinvest most of their profits to sustain their growth. The board of directors will only decide to pay dividends only when the company has achieved a sustainable level of success. Meanwhile, the need to distribute dividends will compel the management to be more responsible.

4. Hedge Against Inflation

Inflation is the main enemy of earnings from stock investments. A moderate inflation rate could take a huge bite out of your profits. Even if you earn a 10% return, a 3% inflation can result to only 7% earnings. Dividends can offset this loss. As companies increase their prices because of inflation, they will earn more money and pay higher dividends.

5. Baby Boomer Boost

The price for dividend stocks could go up as the demand for it will increase because of baby boomers reaching retirement and seeking sources of supplemental income. While this is somewhat of an expert projection, it is still a projection and there's no guarantee that this will really happen. However, the probability of this happening is much higher.

6. Positive Returns in Bear Markets

Companies that are paying dividends will still pay its dues even in bear markets when share prices are dropping or flat. The dividends can help in offsetting any loss from a fall in share prices and there are cases that the results are even positive.

7. Two Ways to Make a Profit

The returns from the dividend stocks could increase when companies pay dividends and when the share prices increase. The only way you can earn positive returns from non-dividend stocks is via appreciation of share price - selling high and buying low.

8. Cash to Purchase More Shares

Once you purchase a certain number of shares of a non-dividend company, you can obtain that certain number of shares. If you like to acquire more shares, you need to use your own money to buy additional units. If you invest in dividend stocks, you can buy additional shares through reinvestment of all or some of your dividends. There is no need to use your money in your pocket to buy more shares. Most investors are also enrolled in special programs, which allow them to automatically reinvest their dividends.

9. Ownership Retention and Profit Collection

Among the most disappointing attributes of owning shares of non-dividend stock is that all your profits are locked in the investment. You can only access your profits by selling some of your shares. Through dividend stocks, you can retain ownership of the company while still collecting your returns.

While dividend stocks pose less risk compared to non-dividend stocks they also carry some risk and may not be suitable for all types of investors. Aside from the benefits, you should also understand the drawbacks of dividend investing. This will help you decide if this type of stock market investment is really right for you.

Each time you sign an investment agreement with an intermediary such as a mutual fund manager or a broker, you will usually read a lengthy disclaimer about the results not guaranteed. To put this simply, you may earn money from your investments today, but there is no certainty that it will be the same case tomorrow. Just like any other kind of investment, dividend investing also carries some risk.

Disadvantages of Dividend Investing

1. High Dividend Payout Risk

Investing in stocks with a high dividend payout ratio comes with risk. Take note that the company's dividend payout ratio reflects how much of its profits are used to reinvest in growth, pay its debts, serve as cash reserve versus how much is being paid to shareholders.

It can be a delicate balancing act for most companies to figure out the percentage of its profits to allocate for dividends. They surely like to entice and retain investors with high payouts, but also need to keep enough of their earnings to support further growth, and, at the same time, maintain their capacity to raise dividend in the future.

In reality, once the dividend payout ratio of a company becomes too high for sustainability, this can force the business to reduce or cancel payouts altogether.

2. Dividend Policy Changes

Dividend policy refers to the company's plan for figuring out its amount for dividends and any possible increases based on projected earnings. Once a company makes changes to the policy, specifically those that result in reducing or canceling payouts, it will have adverse effect on its share price.

Based on the clientele effect theory the price of a stock is strongly connected to the reaction of investors to policy changes of the company. So when these changes happen, many investors will purchase or sell their company shares.

When a company is forced to cancel its dividends for any reason, you may lose your passive income.

3. Double Taxation

Another disadvantage of investing in dividend stocks is that the payouts are subject to double taxation.
First, you need to pay tax when you receive your payouts because the company issuing the dividends from its net profit has to pay tax on its yearly earnings. These earnings generate the dividend payments of the company.

Second, you need to pay tax again as you receive the payouts as personal income that you have earned over the course of a certain tax year.

Therefore, you are paying tax twice as an individual and as a part owner or a company.

In general, dividend investing is less risky compared to non-dividend stock investing. However, before you can maximize the returns from this type of investment, you need to be very familiar with both the benefits and drawbacks before you buy your first shares.

Managing Risks in Dividend Investing

There is always risk in stock market investing due in part to it unpredictable and variable nature. That being said, there are several factors that can increase risk, some are within your control and some are not.

Even though we cannot eliminate the risk, it is still possible to minimize our exposure by becoming more aware of the factors the influence the market behavior. As a saavy investor, you can manage the risks in dividend investing by dealing with factors that you can control.

1. Diversifying Your Investments

You must never invest all your money in one company stock regardless of how promising the business is. Its competitors may dominate the market. The management may be corrupt or incompetent. Or the firm or its whole industry may lose the favor of investors for any reason. These are beyond your control.

The good thing is that you have absolute control over where you want to pour your money. You can greatly minimize the risk by spreading your stock investments in different stocks.

2. Minimize Human Error

Human error is the largest risk factor with dividend investing, and it may result from the following:

- Lack of knowledge
- Misaligned investment strategy and investment goals
- Insufficient research and analysis
- Using emotions over logic in choosing stocks
- Failure to keep track of market conditions
- Allowing panic and fear influence investment decisions

Doing your due diligence is the best way to eliminate human error. You certainly know the risk involved in not being prepared if you have taken an exam you have not studied for. Aside from the unsettling feeling of having not knowing the right answers, you will experience panic that will not help your situation.

3. Use Reason Over Emotion

The Efficient Market Hypothesis is one of the prevailing theories about the mechanics behind the stock market. This hypothesis describes investors as logical people who are capable of understanding all available information in the market to make reasonable decisions for maximum profits. However, most people are not logical or rational.

Many investors are buying stocks based on advice from their family or friends and sometimes from people they don't know. Some investors buy or sell their stocks because of what they heard over the news, or because a new company is making a product they adore and they are sure that it will be a big hit in the market. They know nothing about the history of the stock, its management, or the company as a whole.

To effectively manage the risks in dividend investing, it is best to avoid these three major emotions: Love, Fear, and Greed

Love:

You must never fall in love with your investments. Remember, these are lifeless things that are not capable of loving you back. But it is interesting that they can betray you and hurt you.
Some investors are so in love with the company they hold stocks in that they refuse to sell even when indicators show that the company's inherent value has deteriorated and the share price is falling. You need to bail out when a stock declines sharply.

Review your stocks regularly and scrutinize each investment on its recent performance. If it is not contributing to your portfolio's growth, you can sell your shares, which you can easily do because stocks are very liquid.

Fear:

Investors who experienced losing money in the stock market are susceptible to fear that it paralyzes them from taking any action. Rather than taking on some risk with high potential investments, they are putting their money in safe investments with low rates of return.

Greed

Greed is the opposite of fear. Most investors who have made a lot of money in the stock market would usually want more.

Some investors are vulnerable to the bandwagon effect, pouring their money into the "hottest" companies and industries. This inflates a bubble that will eventually burst.

Greedy investors usually tend to invest in instruments they don't fully understand or they can't afford and then fall into the trap of increasing their investments to recover their losses.

Interesting Fact #2

Dividend investors also love a company that has a history of boosting its dividend. Only a handful of companies are elite enough to join what's referred to as the Dividend Aristocrats club -- those companies that have raised their dividend for 25 or more consecutive years. No company, though, is more elite than ATM and security systems manufacturer **Diebold** (NYSE:DBD), which earlier this year increased its dividend for a record 60th consecutive year.

Chapter 2

Key Technical Terms

Remember, one success ingredient for generating profits in dividend investing is due diligence. And before you even scrutinize each stock that you want to buy and include in your stock market portfolio, you should first learn the key technical terms that you will surely encounter in this field.

In this Chapter, we will briefly discuss some of the technical terms you will encounter while assessing each stock for your dividend investment.

Payout Ratio

Payout Ratio, also known as the Dividend Payout Ratio, refers to the **proportion of profits issued as dividends** to shareholders. This is usually expressed as a percentage, but can also be expressed as a cash flow proportion.

To determine the Payout Ratio, you can use the following formula:

(Total Paid Dividends / Net Income) x 100 = Payout Ratio

or

(Dividends Per Share (DPS) / Earnings Per Share (EPS)) x 100 = Payout Ratio

By the end of a certain period, usually at the end of a fiscal year, some companies issue payout dividends. The source of the dividend is the *net earnings* of the company and represent a return to shareholders.

The payout ratio is an important financial metric that is used to figure out the sustainability of the dividend payments of a company. This is the number of dividends issued to shareholders that is relevant to the total net income of the firm.

For instance, ABC Company with profits per share of $2 and dividends per share of $0.70 has a payout ratio of 35 percent. XYZ Company with profits per share of $2 and dividends per share of $1 has a ratio of 50 percent. So which of these two companies has a more sustainable payout ratio.

It really depends on the sector because there is no single number that can define a suitable payout ratio.

Companies in cyclical industries like energy and resources **usually have lower dividends** because their profits are not constant and dependent on the economic cycle. Hence, the name.

On the other hand, companies in defensive industries like telecommunications, pipelines, and utilities have predictable and stable profits and cash flows and **could support much higher payouts compared to cyclical sectors.**

In our earlier example, if ABC Company is a commodity producer and Company XYZ is a regulated firm, XYZ's payout sustainability may be better compared to ABC, even though ABC has a lower absolute payout ratio compared to XYZ.

Some companies only pay out a percentage of their profits, while some pay out all of their profits to shareholders. If the company is paying out some of the profits as dividends, it will keep the rest of the portion.

Retention ratio (which you will learn a bit later) will allow you to measure the level of earnings retained by the company.

A reduced payout ratio signifies that the company is using more of its profits to operate or to grow the company. In this case, the retention ratio will be higher.

A high payout ratio could mean that the company is sharing more of its profits with its shareholders. The retention ratio will be lower in this case.

A payout ratio higher than 100 percent signifies that the company is paying out more dividends compared to its earning. While this may seem good for investors, this move is not sustainable.

Companies who are regularly issuing dividend payouts have a target range for their payout ratios and define them as cash flow or sustainable earnings.

A stable payout ratio over the years signifies that the company has a viable record of dividend payouts.

Many blue-chip companies have stable payout ratios over the years despite their dividend increases.

Retention Ratio

Retention Ratio, also known as Plowback Ratio, refers to the percentage of profits retained by the company. This percentage is called retained profits.

Instead of distributing as dividends, the company may choose to retain the earnings to further expand business operations, start a new project, or acquire new assets.

Retention Ratio is the opposite of the Payout Ratio, which measures the proportion of profits distributed to stockholders as dividends.

Use the following formula to determine the company's Retention Ratio:

(Net Income - Dividends) / Net Income = Retention Ratio

For a per-share basis, this ratio can be also expressed as:

1 - (Dividends Per Share / Earnings Per Share)

Dividend Yield

Dividend Yield refers to the ratio of the company's yearly dividend in comparison to its share price. This figure is expressed in percentage and can be determined using the following formula:

Yearly Dividend / Share Price = Dividend Yield

The yearly dividend used in the formula can be the most recent dividend x 4, the total dividend paid over the past four quarters, or the total dividends issued by the company during the most recent fiscal year.

The dividend yield can also signify the dividend-only return of investment. The yield will fall if the price of the stock rises, and it will rise if the price of the stock falls assuming the dividend is not lowered or raised.

This usually looks high for stocks that are quickly falling because the dividend yield has an inverse relationship with the share price.

Let's say that the stock of Company M is trading at $20 and yield a yearly dividend of $1 for every share. Meanwhile, let's say that the stock of Company H is trading at $40 and yields a yearly dividend of $1 for every share.

Using the formula above, we can say that the dividend yield of Company M is at 5 percent (1/20=0.05), while the dividend yield of Company H is only 2.5 percent (1/40=0.025).

All other factors being equal, the better choice is Company M because it has twice the dividend yield compared to Company H.

Although high dividend yields are enticing, they can affect the potential growth cost. The money that the company is issuing as dividends to stockholders is the money that the company cannot use for generating capital gains or for expansion. Stockholders can earn more returns if the value of their stock grows while they are holding their units.

Historical data reveals that a concentration on dividends can boost returns instead of slowing them down.

Based on a study conducted by Hartford Funds, more than 82% of the total returns since 1960 from S&P 500 are from dividends. This has traction because it operates under the assumption that investors are willing to reinvest their dividends to the company. This significantly compounds their capacity to earn more money in the long-term.

Basically, established companies that are no longer expanding fast enough tend to have the most dividend yields. Companies that are in utilities or staple industries are good examples of industries that are paying the best average dividend yield.

In tech stocks, the average dividend yield is lower. But the rule about established companies also applies to the same sector.

It is also important to take note that the **dividend yield cannot tell you much about what type of dividend that a company is paying**. For instance, the dividend yield in the market is highest with REITs (Real Estate Investment Trusts). But these are from ordinary dividends that are a bit different compared to the traditional qualified dividends.

BDCs (Business Development Companies) and MLPs (Master Limited Partnerships) also have very high average dividend yields. These business organizations are all required by the government to pass through most of their profits to shareholders.

Concerns with Dividend Yields

It is not safe to assess a stock based solely on the dividend yield simply because dividend data might be obsolete or based on erroneous data.

Most companies have a very high yield as their stock plummets. This usually occurs before cutting the dividend payout.

You can use the most recent financial report of a company to compute its dividend yield. This is fine during the first quarter after the company has released its yearly financial report.

This information will no longer be reliable if you need data for 2nd to the 4th quarter. As an alternative, you can get the total of the last four quarters of dividends that can cover the trailing year of dividend data. Using this data can be good, but may not be enough if the dividend has been raised or cut.

Most companies are paying dividends every quarter. So, investors are taking the last quarterly dividend, multiply it by 4 and use the result as the yearly dividend. This method can reflect any recent change in the dividend. However, not all companies pay a uniform dividend every quarter.

Some companies - especially non-US organizations - choose to pay a minimal quarterly dividend than a large dividend at the end of a fiscal year. Therefore, you may get an inflated dividend yield if you perform the computation after the distribution of the yearly dividend.

Some companies are also issuing payouts more regularly than every quarter. Therefore, using the figure for a monthly dividend will result in too low a dividend yield.

In choosing how to compute the dividend yield, you should look at the record of dividend payouts to choose the most suitable approach that will provide you the most reliable results.

You should also be cautious in assessing a company that seems distressed with a higher dividend yield. Remember, the share price is the denominator of the formula for dividend yield. So, a strong fall in the price may significantly bloat the quotient.

Ex-Dividend

Ex-dividend refers to the stock that is trading devoid of the value for the next dividend payout. The day that the stock begins trading without the value of the next dividend payout is known as the ex-dividend date or ex-date.

If you buy a stock on or after the ex-dividend date, you are not entitled to the announced dividend. **If you buy a stock *before* the ex-dividend date, you are entitled to the payout.**

The stock normally drops in price by the amount of the expected payout because buyers are not entitled to the next payout on the ex-date.

Once a company decides to issue a dividend payout, the board of directors will determine a record date. You should take note of the record date because this is when you should be on the company's list as a stockholder so you can receive the dividend payout.

After establishing the record date, the ex-dividend date is also set based on the rules of the stock exchange on which the stock will be traded. Hence, the ex-dividend date is usually one business day prior to the record date.

For instance, when a company announced a dividend on 3 June with a record date on Monday, July 11, the ex-dividend date will be 8 July Friday because this is one business day prior to the ex-dividend date.

The ex-dividend date happens before the record date because of the manner stock trades are paid. Once a trade happens, the record of this transaction is not paid for two more business days. This is called the T+2 payment. Hence, if you own the stocks on 7 July but sold the stocks on 8 July, you are still a shareholder of the company based on the record because the trade is not yet complete. But if you sold your shares on 7 July, then the trade would be settled by 11 July, and the new owner will be entitled to the dividend payout.

There are some slight changes when the company decides to issue a dividend in stock rather than cash. With stock dividends, the ex-dividend date will be recorded on the first business day after the settlement of the dividend.

Let's say, ABC company declared in a press release dated 8 April 2017, that it will start trading ex-dividend on 8 April. The record date was determined as 9 April. Prior to this, the company already announced the dividend payout of $0.62 per share scheduled for 2 May, so stockholders who bought the stocks from the company before the ex-date of 8 April will be entitled to the cash payment.

Importance of Knowing Ex-Dividend Date

Understanding the mechanics behind and around ex-dividend payment is crucial. You need to purchase a dividend-paying stock at least two days prior to the record date because it will take two days to settle the trade.

Knowing when the ex-date happens can help you plan your trade entries, especially if your investing strategy is focused on income. But because the price of the stock drops by about the equal value of the payout, purchasing shares before the ex-dividend payment is unlikely to yield any profits. Likewise, investors purchasing stocks on the ex-dividend date or after *can take advantage of a lower share price.*

The Movement of Stock Price on the Ex-Dividend Date

By average, a stock could drop by a bit less than the dividend payout. The fluctuation triggered by small dividend is quite difficult to detect because the stock prices are moving daily. It is easier to observe the movements of the stock prices during large dividend payouts.

The ex-dividend date is surrounded by other crucial dates in the process for dividend distribution.

Record Date

This date refers to the exact date that the company is reviewing its list of shareholders. This is usually one day after the ex-dividend date. However, this is not a primary deciding factor for dividend investing.

Declaration Date

Also called announcement date, the declaration date refers to the date when the company announces dividend payout. This is an important date because any changes in the payout may cause the share price to fluctuate as traders are still adjusting their investments based on the news.

Payment Date

This is the date when dividend payouts are credited or checks are sent to investor accounts. Because the payment date is known prior to this, the event must not have any effect on the price of the stocks.

Price-Earnings Ratio (P/E Ratio)

P/E Ratio refers to the ratio for valuing a business organization that measures its present stock price relative to the per-share profits. This is also known as the earnings multiple or the price multiple.

Below is the formula used for calculating the P/E ratio:

Market Value per Share / Earnings per Share

In general, the P/E ratio indicates the dollar amount that an investor is expecting to invest in a company so it can receive a dollar off from the company's profits. This is the reason why this ratio is also called the price multiple because *it will show you how much investors are willing to pay for every dollar of profits.* If a company is presently trading at a multiple (P/E) of 15, this indicates that an investor is willing to pay $15 for a dollar of the present profits.

The EPS (Earnings Per Share) should be known to calculate the P/E ratio. The EPS is usually derived from the last four quarters. This type of P/E ratio is known as the trailing P/E that can be calculated by finding the difference between the share value of the company at the start of the 12-month period from its value at the end.

There are also instances that the price-earnings can also be taken from the estimates of the profits projected during the next four quarters. This type of price-earnings is known as a forward or projected P/E. Another form of P/E uses the sum of the estimates for the next two quarters and the figures from the last two actual quarters.

Basically, a high P/E indicates that investors are projecting higher profits growth in the future in comparison with companies with lower P/E. On the other hand, a lower P/E can signify that a company might be undervalued at present or that the company is doing great well relative to its historical trends. If a company is posting losses or has no profits, in both cases, P/E is written as N/A. While it is possible to get a negative P/E, this is very rare.

P/E Ratio is also considered as a way for standardizing the value of one dollar of profits in the stock market. Theoretically, you can get the median of P/E ratios over a certain period so you can establish a standard P/E ratio. You can use this as a benchmark to guide you with regards to whether a certain stock is ideal to buy.

Limitations of the P/E Ratio

Similar to any other fundamentals designed to guide investors in buying stocks, the P/E Ratio has its limits that you should consider. Be that as it may, please be aware that there is no *single metric* that can provide you with an absolute insight into your investment decision.

One major limitation of using P/E ratio rises in comparing P/E ratios of various companies. Growth rates and valuations of companies may usually vary wildly between sectors because of the different ways that companies are earning money to the different timelines during which organizations are earning their profits.

Therefore, you should only use Price-Earnings Ratio as a tool for comparison when you are *considering companies in the same industry*. This type of comparison is the only type that can provide you with reliable insight. Your assumptions will not be highly reliable if you compare the P/E ratios of an energy company and a media company.

Comparing the P/E ratios of several companies in the same sector is much more meaningful. For instance, a telecommunications company may have high P/E ratio, but this might be an indication of a trend in the sector instead of one emerging from that specific company. If the entire industry has high P/E ratios, the high P/E ratio of a single company in that industry may be less of a concern.

Furthermore, because the debt of a company could affect both its profits and prices of shares, leverage can also affect the P/E ratios. Let's say that there are two companies in the same sector. They have a different take on their payables. Company A has lower debt and has a lower P/E ratio than Company B that has higher debt. But if the industry is doing well, Company B has the higher potential to earn more mainly due to the risks it has taken.

Another major limitation of P/E ratio is one that dwells inside the equation used to figure out P/E itself. Objective and accurate presentations of P/E ratio could depend on accurate inputs of the market value of shares as well as accurate earnings for share estimates.

Even though the market establishes the value of shares and so this information is available from different reliable references this is less likely to happen for profits that are usually reported by companies and so they are not completely reliable. Because profits are an essential input for computing P/E, changing them can also change the P/E ratio.

Here are the things you need to remember when you are looking into the P/E ratios of company stocks you want to buy:
- The average market P/E ratio is 20 to 25x profits
- A high P/E ratio signifies that investors are projecting higher growth for the company
- Companies that are losing money don't have P/E ratio
- Estimated profits can be used to obtain the forward-looking price-earnings ratio

Dividend Growth Rate

Dividend growth rate refers to the yearly growth of the percentage rate that a specific stock's dividend experiences over a specific period of time.

This metric is crucial for using the dividend discount model, which is a form of security pricing model. This operates under the assumption that the estimated future dividends will determine the price of a given stock discounting the excess of internal growth over the estimated dividend growth of a company.

Using this model, a certain stock could be considered as undervalued if the outcome is higher compared to the current price of the share of the company. You can figure out the intrinsic value of a certain stock if you estimate the expected value of cash flow using the dividend discount model.

A record of stable dividend growth may signify future dividend growth that also indicates profitability for a specific company. If you calculate the dividend growth rate, you can use any interval time you want. You can also compute the dividend growth rate using the least squares approach or just by looking at the yearly figure over a specific period.

How to Compute the Dividend Growth Rate

You can determine the dividend growth rate by taking an average using the linear method. For example, let's say that a company issued the following dividend payments to its stockholders over the last 5 years:

2014 = $1.00
2015 = $1.05
2016 = $1.07
2017 = $1.11
2018 = $1.15

To determine the growth from 2014 to 2018, you can use the formula below:

Year X Dividend / (Year X - 1 Dividend) - 1 = Dividend Growth

The following are the growth rates for our example above:

2014 Growth Rate = N/A
2015 Growth Rate = $1.05 / $1.00 - 1 = 5%
2016 Growth Rate = $1.07 / $1.05 - 1 = 1.9%
2017 Growth Rate = $1.11 / $1.07 - 1 = 3.74%
2018 Growth Rate = $1.15 / $1.11 - 1 = 3.6%

The average yearly growth for the company is 3.56%.

Meanwhile, you can use the dividend discount model to value the stock of a company. This model is based on the concept that a stock will be worth the sum of the future payments to stockholders that is discounted back to the current date.

The formula uses three variables to obtain the current price (P). These are:

r = equity capital cost
D1 = dividend value for next year
g = the growth rate of the dividend

The formula for the dividend discount model is:

$$P = D1 / (r-g)$$

Using the example above, if the dividend for 2019 will be $1.18 and the equity capital cost is 8%, the price of the stock for every share will be $26.58 as shown in the equation below:

$$P = \$1.18 / (8\%-3.56\%) = \$26.58$$

Return On Equity (ROE)

Return on Equity (ROE) is a metric of financial performance that can be determined by getting the ratio of the net income and equity of the shareholders. This metric is considered as the return on net assets because the equity of the shareholders is equal to the assets of the company less its debt.

ROE is written as a percentage and can be computed for any company if equity and net income are both positive numbers. Net income is computed prior to the payout of common stocks and after the payout of preferred stocks on top of lender interests.

Low or high ROE will dramatically vary from one sector to another. *The comparison will be more meaningful if you use this metric to assess one company to another company in the same sector*. But take note that even with the same sector, comparing the ROE of a company that is paying a huge dividend with a firm that doesn't pay dividend could be misleading.

Trailing 12 months or the net income over the last fiscal year can be found in the income statement, which will provide you an overview of the company's financial activity over this period.

On the other hand, the balance sheet will show the equity of the shareholders. This balance sheet refers to the running balance of the organization's whole history of changes in liabilities and assets. It is ideal to compute ROE based on the average equity over this period because of the mismatch between the income statement and the balance sheet.

ROE = Net Income / Average Shareholder Equity

The average equity of a shareholder is computed by adding equity at the start of the period to equity at the end and dividing by 2. You can use the balance sheets (quarterly) to come up with a more reliable equity average.

Let's say that Company XYZ has a yearly income of $1,900,000. The average equity of shareholders stands at $15,000,000. The ROE of this company would be 12.6%.

It is not ideal to compare the ROE of two companies if they are not the same. But some investors consider this metric near the long-term average of 10 to 15% as an ideal ratio. Meanwhile, anything that is lower than 10% will be considered poor ROE.

The Role of ROE in Determining the Growth Rate

Even though there could be some concerns, ROE can be a good starting point for projecting the future estimates of the growth rate of stock as well as the dividend's growth rate. These two metrics could be employed to make comparison easier between companies that are within the same industry.

To get the estimate of the future growth rate of a company, you can multiply ROE by the retention ratio of the company. The retention ratio refers to the percentage of net income that is reinvested or retained by the company to fuel its growth.

Let's say that two companies, YumTime and TacoMadness both have the same net income and ROE, but different retention ratios. The ROE of YumTime is 15% while its returns are at 30% of its net income to shareholders in a dividend. This means that the company is reinvesting 70% of its net profit.

On the other hand, TacoMadness also has an ROE of 15% but only issues 10% of its profits to its shareholders, which means that the company is reinvesting 90% of its profits for growth.

YumTime Growth Rate is 10.5% because:

15% (ROE) x 70% (Retention Ratio) = 10.5%

TacoMadness Growth Rate is 13.5% because:

15% (ROE) X 90% (Retention Ratio) = 13.5 %

This assessment is known as the *sustainable growth model*, which you can use to estimate the future of a specific company and determine stocks that can be risky because they are going over the sustainable growth ability.

A company that has a slow growth rate compared to its sustainable rate might be undervalued, or the stock market is just ignoring the red flags. In both cases, the growth rate that is below or above the sustainable rate requires deeper due diligence.

By earlier assessment, TacoMadness may seem more enticing compared to YumTime. However, this ignores the benefits of a higher dividend rate that can attract investors. You can change the calculation to make the estimate of the dividend growth rate of the stock that could be more essential for investors who are looking for regular passive income.

By multiplying ROE by the payout ratio, you can get an estimate of the dividend growth rate. The payout ratio refers to the portion of net income that is issued to common stockholders via dividends. This approach can provide us the sustainable dividend growth rate that makes YumTime more attractive:

YumTime Growth Rate is 4.5% because:

15% (ROE) x 30% (Payout Ratio) = 4.5%

TacoMadness Growth Rate is 1.5% because:

15% (ROE) x 10% (Payout Ratio) = 1.5%

A stock that is showing growth beyond its sustainable rate may indicate some red flags that should be thoroughly investigated.

Using ROE for Stock Comparison

A bad or good ROE will largely depend on what is common for the peers of the stock. For instance, companies in the utility sector usually have big asset and debt accounts on the balance sheet in comparison to a small amount of net profit. The common ROE for a utility company could be 10% or even lower.

On the other hand, companies in the retail industry usually have smaller balance sheet accounts that are relative to net income but may have ROE of 18% or even higher.

As a reference, you can target companies with ROE that is equal or just a bit above the average for the sector. For instance, let's say a company TechX has sustained the 18% ROE over five years in comparison to other companies in the industry that only sustained 15%. You may say that the company's management is a lot more efficient at using its assets to generate income.

Using ROE to Spot Red Flags

Many investors often wonder why a stock with an above average ROE is good instead of a company that has double the average of other companies in the same sector. In the first place, companies with very high ROE seems to have higher value.

There are cases when very high ROE can be a good thing if the net income is extremely large in comparison with the equity because the performance of a company can be strong. But more often than not, high ROE is caused by a small equity account in comparison to net income that signifies risk.

Negative ROE

ROE is often not calculated if a company has a negative income. However, ROE can be negative if the company has negative equity because of a prior period of losses, long-term pattern of share buybacks or excessive borrowings. The denominator in the computation, in this case, will result in a negative number.

The most common concern with negative ROE is *inconsistent profitability or excessive debt*. But there are exceptions to this rule for companies that are profitable and have been using their profits to purchase their own shares.

For some companies, this is an alternative way of issuing dividends and it could reduce the equity enough to make the ROE negative.

As an investor, you should investigate further if you encounter stocks with high or negative ROE. In rare circumstances, a negative ROE ratio might be caused by efficient management and cash flow supported share buyback scheme.

Also, take note that companies with negative ROE should not be assessed against other companies with positive ROE.

Inconsistent Profits

Let's say you are evaluating a company that is not making money for three years now. The losses are recorded on the balance sheet in the equity portion and tagged as a retained loss.

The losses have reduced shareholder equity and resulted in a negative value. But this year, the company landed a huge project that boosted its profitability. After this windfall, the denominator in the ROE formula will be very small considering the company has been losing money. This makes the ROE of the company high and unreliable.

For trained investors, the high ROE of the company will signify that it has no profitable track record in the past four years. Investing in this stock would be riskier compared to those with lower ROE and consistent profit trends.

High Debt

Companies that are aggressively borrowing can increase ROE because equity is equal to assets less debt. Higher debt may result in lower equity.

A usual scenario that may cause this concern happens when a company is borrowing huge amounts of debt to purchase its own stock. This could boost the company's earnings per share but it will not affect its performance or actual growth rates.

Looking at ROE in comparing stocks can be helpful, but *you should be careful in comparing stocks with different dividend strategies or stocks of companies that operate in different industries.*

Debt Equity (D/E) Ratio

You can determine D/E Ratio by dividing the total liabilities of a company by its shareholder equity. You can find these figures on the balance sheet of a company you are evaluating.

The D/E Ratio is used to assess the financial leverage of the company. This is also known as the gearing ratio. Below is the formula for computing the D/E Ratio:

$$\text{Debt/Equity Ration} = \text{Total Liabilities/Total Shareholder Equity}$$

In the balance sheet, the assets should be equal the total shareholder equity less the liabilities. This is an alternative form of the balance sheet formula (Shareholder Equity + Liabilities = Assets).

These balance sheet categories may contain individual accounts that are usually considered "equity" or "debt" in the conventional form. Take note that the ratio can be affected by pension plan adjustments, intangible assets, retained earnings/losses.

Better due diligence is required so you can fully understand the true leverage of the company. Some of the accounts in the main balance sheet categories tend to be ambiguous, so you may need to modify the D/E ratio to be more viable and easier to compare between different assets.

You can also improve your assessment of the D/E Ratio by including growth expectations, profit performance, and short-term leverage ratios.

How to Use D/E Ratio for Corporate Fundamental Analysis

Because the D/E Ratio is used to measure the debt of the company relative to the net value of its assets, this is often used to measure the extent to which the company is taking on debt as a way of leveraging its assets.

High D/E Ratio is usually associated with high risk. This signifies that the company is aggressive in funding its growth using debt.

At the end of 2018, ArrowStrike had total liabilities of $43.54 billion, total shareholder equity of $31.9 billion, and a D/E Ratio Of 1.36. On the other hand, Orinoco Inc had total liabilities of $13.2 billion, total shareholder equity of $8.80 billion and a D/E ratio of 1.50 at the end of the year.

ArrowStrike: $43.54 / $31.9 = 1.36
Orinoco Inc: $13.2 / $8.80 = 1.50

In fast assessment, it may appear that the higher leverage ratio of Orinoco Inc signifies higher risk. But this conclusion can be too generalized and more due diligence is in order.
If the company is using debt to finance its growth, it would possibly earn more profits than it would have without the debt. If the leverage can boost the profits by a higher amount compared to the interest (cost of debt), then stockholder will benefit.

However, if the interest outweighs the income generated the share values may fall. The interest may vary with market conditions, so unprofitable debt may not be significant at first.

Adjustments in assets and long-term debt tend to have the biggest effect on the D/E ratio because they are often bigger accounts compared to short-term assets and debt.

If you want to assess the short-term leverage of the company and its capacity to pay its debt for a fiscal year, you can use other ratios and metrics.

For instance, if you need to compare the solvency or the short-term liquidity, you can use the current ratio (short-term liabilities + short-term assets) or the cash ratio (short term liabilities + cash and marketable securities) rather than the long-term measure of leverage such as D/E ratio.

Limits of D/E Ratio

It is crucial to look into the sector of the company you are evaluating if you are using D/E ratio. Because various sectors have various growth rates and capital needs, a high ratio might be common in one sector, while a low ratio may be common in another.

For instance, tech companies usually have D/E ratio under 0.5, while capital-intensive sectors such as auto manufacturing tend to have a ratio above 2.

Utility companies usually have a very high ratio in comparison to market averages. A utility has a lower growth rate but is often able to sustain a constant income stream that allows these companies to borrow at a lower interest rate.

High leverage ratios in slow growth sectors with steady profits signify efficient capital use. The non-cyclical consumer sector tends to also have high D/E ratio because these companies have a stable income and can borrow money at a lower interest rate.

You should take note that not all stock analysts are consistent about debt. For instance, preferred stock is often considered as equity, while the liquidation rights, par value, and preferred dividend make this form of equity look a lot more like debt.

Adding preferred stock in total debt may increase the D/E ratio and make a company less attractive. Adding preferred stock in the equity portion of the ratio can lower the ratio and increase the denominator. This can be a huge issue for companies such as real estate investment trusts (REITs) when preferred stock is added in the D/E ratio.

Let's say that Avante Inc has $1.2 million in total shareholder equity (excluding preferred stock), $1 million in total debt (excluding preferred stock), and has $500k in preferred stock.

D/E ratio with preferred stock as part of total liabilities:
Debt/Equity Ratio 1.25 = ($1m + $500k)/$1.25m

D/E ratio with preferred stock as part of shareholder equity:
Debt/Equity Ratio 0.57 = $1m/($1.25m + $500k)

Other financial accounts like unearned profits will be categorized as debt and may distort the D/E ratio. Let's look at a company with a prepaid contract to build a new warehouse for $2 million. Because the work is not complete, so the $2 million is still categorized as a liability. On record, the company has purchased $1 million of materials and inventory to complete the project that has increased shareholder equity and total assets.

If you include these figures in the D/E computation, the numerator will be increased by $2 million while the denominator by $1 million that will increase the ratio.

Changes to D/E Ratio

The total value of assets less liabilities is equal to the equity portion of shareholders. However, this is not the same thing as assets less the debt associated with the assets. The conventional approach to resolving this issue is to change the D/E ratio into the long-term D/E ratio. This approach can help you focus on essential risks.

The overall leverage of a company still includes short-term debt, which is moderately risky because these are often settled within a year or shorter. Consider the following figures of two companies in the manufacturing industry:

Company A: $500,000 (long-term debt) and $1 million short term debt (notes, accounts payable, and wages)
Company B: $1 million (long-term debt) and $500,000 (short-term payables).

Both companies will have a D/E ratio if they both have $1.5 million in shareholder equity. At first look, the leverage risk of these two companies can be similar, but further assessment will come up with Company B as less risky.

In general, short-term debt has the tendency to be more affordable compared to long-term debt and it is less sensitive to changing interest rates. So the cost of capital and interest expense of Company A is higher. Higher debt cost would seem to make the company more attractive with more long-term debt. However, it is still at a disadvantage if the debt can be redeemed through bonds.

Dividend Coverage Ratio (DCR)

DCR is another important metric in stock investing. It states the number of times an organization is capable of paying dividends to shareholders from the profits earned during an accounting period.

You can figure out the dividend coverage ratio by dividing the net income by the dividend issued to stockholders.

Dividend Coverage Ratio = Net Income / Dividend Payout

The net income refers to the company earnings *after paying all expenses* including taxes. On the other hand, Dividend Payout refers to the amount of dividend entitled to stockholders.
There are some modified forms of the DCR that we will discuss in this book.
The first form of DCR is used to figure out the number of times that a company can issue dividends to common stockholders if the company also has preferred stockholders to consider. Below is the formula for this variation:

DCR = (Net Income - Required Preferred Dividend Payouts) / Dividends Issued to Common Stockholders

This form is also used to figure out the number of times that a company can issue dividends to preferred stockholders: Below is the formula:

DCR = Net Income / Dividends Issued to Preferred Stockholders

Example of DCR

For our example, let's take a look at a company that has reported the following numbers:

$ 500,000 (income before tax)
30% (tax rate)
$20,000 (dividend paid to preferred stockholders)
$25,000 (dividend paid to common shareholders)

In this case, you can figure out the DCR for common and preferred stockholders

($500,000 x 70%) / $20,000 = 17.5 (DCR for preferred stockholders)
($500,000 x 70% - $20,000) / $25,000 = 13.2 (DCR for common stockholders)

Remember, if the DCR is higher than 1, it signifies that the profits generated by the company are sufficient to issue dividends to shareholders. A DCR that is higher than 2 is a good indicator.

You should review your calculation or the company numbers if the DCR is below 1.5. A falling or consistently low DCR is usually an indicator that the company will lose profits in the future. The company will be incapable of sustaining its present level of dividend payouts.

Concerns with DCR

While DCR is a reliable indicator of dividend payout risk to stockholders, there are several important issues with this metric that you should consider.

First, you should take a closer look at the net income and remember that this is NOT an actual cash flow. In determining the DCR of a company, analysts often use net income in the numerator.

However, this figure doesn't mean that this is the actual cash flow of the company. Hence, a company may report high net profits but still not have the available cash to pay the dividend.

Second, DCR is not a reliable indicator for assessing future risk. Take note that net income can easily change year after year. Hence, getting a high DCR based on the record of the company's performance is not always a reliable indicator of dividend risk in the future.

Nevertheless, the DCR is still commonly used by analysts and investors to estimate the level of risk that is connected in receiving dividends from an investment.

Interesting Fact #3

Dividends have historically played a gigantic role in creating wealth for investors in the United States. In Susanna Kim's owns words from an ABC News report, "Of the S&P 500's nominal total return from 1910 to 2010, dividend yield and dividend growth comprised 90 percent [of] returns for stock holders." I've certainly come across differing figures in other reports, but the message is the same: Compounding long-term dividend growth is a key driver of wealth appreciation.

Chapter 3

Factors to Consider When Investing in Dividend Stocks

Now that you are a bit familiar with the technical terms that you will regularly encounter as you look for stock investments, it is time to look into factors that will help you to further assess the risk of a specific stock.

There are five factors that we will look at:
- Dividend Yield
- Growth Rate of Company's Profits
- The Health of the Company's Balance Sheet
- The Volume of Company's Debt and Sales Performance
- Current Dividend Tax Laws

We'll explore each factor and discuss specific circumstances that you can use to help you with your stock investments.

Dividend Yield

Issuance of dividends is one sign that a company is in good financial health. As discussed in the previous Chapter, Dividend Yield refers to the ratio that signifies the dividend income for every share dividend by the price per share.

So for example, a stock that is priced at $100 each share and issues $5 dividend, the yield is 5%.

If you are looking into stocks for your long-term investment, Dividend Yield is one of the first metrics that you should assess. You can use the dividends to purchase more shares so you don't need to commit more of your own resources just to grow your equity holdings.

Some investors depend on yields to produce a steady stream of income from their stock dividend investments. While not quite as guaranteed as fixed-income investments like bonds, dividend generating stocks could be quite valuable in this way.

But as a savvy investor, you should not only look into the Dividend Yield as this one-sided analysis can easily mislead you. There are companies that choose to continue paying yield even when they are operating at a loss. On the other hand, there are also companies that are paying very high dividends that they are not reinvesting enough to sustain their growth.

Dividend Yield and Total Return

It may be helpful in your assessment to compare Dividend Yield with Total Return. The latter is a direct representation of how much an investment has actually generated for the stockholder.
Dividend Yield only shows the actual cash dividend while the total return includes the interest and increases in share price alongside dividend and other capital gains.

By itself, this seems to provide more insight and so is a useful metric for stock performance compared to Dividend Yield. But the return is completely retrospective as the price of shares may increase for various reasons. It is often more difficult to predict the performance of future investment from the returns of stocks compared to the Dividend Yield.

Choosing between Dividend Yield and Total Return in assessing your possible stock investments can be tricky. Total Return is a more important metric to consider if you need to identify the stocks that have *performed better over a period of time.*

On the other hand, looking into the Dividend Yield is more important if you want to invest in stocks that will *provide you a steady income.*

It is more sensible and reasonable to focus on Total Return if you have a long-term investment plan and you are keen on keeping your equity holdings for several years.

Also, take note that the assessment of a company for possible equity investment must never be confined to these two metrics alone. Instead, you should carefully look at the income statement and balance sheet of the company and never neglect due diligence.

Relative Dividend Yield (RDY) Strategy

RDY Strategy is an important approach if you want to compare the yield of a specific stock to the yield of a sector. This way, you can figure out whether a stock is expensive or underpriced.

This strategy is not recommended for those who are looking for fast returns. This is a long-term strategy that will provide you with substantial results after a minimum of three years.

Moreover, this strategy doesn't depend on P/E ratios, forecasted profits, or past earnings to determine the valuations.

This approach will encourage you to be more contrarian, independent, disciplined and patient. These qualities will help you to concentrate on big companies who might be struggling at present but are already established organizations that are highly capable of recovering.

Employing absolute yield to pinpoint undervalued stocks in the market will leave you with several mature companies in slow-growth sectors.

Investors who are following the RDY strategy are eying for income and capital appreciation. Take note that the yield in this approach doesn't need to be very high (just a bit higher in the market). Hence, it can help you identify possible investment opportunities in both strong and weak markets.

Over the long term, RDY can help you build a portfolio with a higher stream of income (around 1.5 to 2% better total return and lower risk compared to the S&P 500 index.

RDY also signifies the sentiment of investors. A low RDY suggest that investors are enthusiastic about the current market while high RDY signifies market despair.

If you follow this strategy, you can sell dividend stocks when other investors are buying and you can buy dividend stocks when other investors are selling. You can expect the following if you use RDY:

Low Risk

The stocks you have identified through RDY tend to have lower risk than the rest of the companies in the market because these are often stocks that are ignored.

When RDY identifies a possible investment, the stock is already underperforming in the market for quite some time. There is a low possibility that the share price will fall further because it has already experienced a dramatic drop.

High Yield

Stocks identified via RDY have higher average yields. Investors who are using the RDY strategy are trained not to buy stocks until the yield is usually at least 50% higher than the market.

In using RDY, you can identify stocks that are undervalued and are expected to eventually see capital gains when it comes to price. Still, the high yield is more likely to indicate a considerable amount for returns to investors.

Low Turnover

In holding equities for an extended period, you can only sell around a third or quarter of the portfolio in a particular year. This is lower compared to the almost 100% turnover in many mutual funds.

Low turnover could lead to lower transactions costs, which will leave you with more money for investment and generation of better returns. Moreover, lower sales could mean fewer capital gains and lower tax bill.

Long Holding Periods

The usual holding period for stocks determined through RDY is 3 to 5 years. Once the share prices of these stocks recover and move higher, it can cause the relative yield of the stock to drop below the yield in the market, which triggers the sell signal.

Less Volatility

Stock portfolios under RDY usually hold big, established companies who are capable of paying consistent dividends. These stocks are less volatile compared to the general market during bear markets.

The Relative Dividend Yield Strategy can signal when to buy and sell stocks based on yield. This stock investing strategy, however, may seem a bit more complicated compared to the dividend strategy that uses absolute yield.

Growth Rate of Company's Profits

Another factor that you should look into when you are assessing stocks for your dividend investment strategy is the rate of growth in the company's profit. This is an important figure to take a closer look at so you can project future dividend increases.

The revenue and earnings of a company are among the initial metrics that you need to consider in choosing stocks for your dividend investing portfolio.

It can be difficult for a company to ensure growth if its profits are not growing. You should look for stocks of companies that have traction when it comes to increasing the amount of money they are generating in sales.

Aside from the revenue amount, the next figure to look for growth is the earnings of the company. This is also known as the net profit that refers to the amount of money the company retains after paying all its expenses (wages, taxes, and other liabilities).

The company profits are influenced by different factors such as assets, liabilities, financing, and operational expenses. To look for consistent growth in earnings you need to look into Earnings Per Share (EPS) of the company.

What is EPS?

Basically, EPS refers to the amount of net income earned per share of stock outstanding. In other words, this is the amount of money each share of stock would receive if all of the profits were distributed to the outstanding shares at the end of the year. This figure serves as an indicator of the profitability of the company.

In determining the EPS of a company, you need to first look for the weighted average number of common shares, net profit, and dividends paid on preferred shares. You can find all these figures in the income statement and balance sheet of a company.

It is better to use the weighted average number of common shares than the reporting term because the number of shares may change over time. Take note that any splits or stock dividends should be included in the computation of the weighted average number of outstanding shares.

A crucial aspect of EPS that is usually ignored is the capital needed to generate the net profits in the computation. Two companies may show the same EPS number, but one can do so with lower net assets. Such a company would be considered more efficient in using its capital in generating income and would be a more attractive investment.

Even though EPS is widely used as a way to monitor the performance of a company, shareholders don't have direct access to these earnings. A percentage of these earnings may be issued as a dividend, but a percentage of the EPS will be reserved by the company.

In order to access more of these profits, shareholders through their representatives in the company may decide to change the portion of EPS allocated for dividends.

Because stockholders cannot access the EPS allocated to their shares, the link between the share price and EPS may be difficult to identify. This is often true for companies that are not paying dividends.

Increasing Profits = Increasing Dividends

Once a company decides to enter a cycle of rising dividends, its management will be highly motivated to keep the trend. The board of directors will always pressure the management to increase the profits and ensure that the cash flow each year will be enough to pay dividends and retain sufficient earnings to fund its growth.

Without traction of increasing profits, the company may be forced to decrease or even cancel its dividend payouts. This will often cause the share price to drop sharply in the stock market. Moreover, company executives are under pressure to avoid hurting the stock price because they are usually compensated in cash and in stock options.

The company's track record of growing its dividends in the past is one strong indicator that a company has the capacity to grow its dividends in the future. Another indicator is a low payout ratio, which is the ratio of dividends to profits.

The Health of the Company's Balance Sheet

In considering an investment opportunity, stock analysts begin by assessing the balance sheet of a company. The balance sheet will provide you with a snapshot of the company's assets and liabilities in a given period of time.

Numbers don't lie especially when it comes to dividend investing. Many investors look into the cash or the top line, which is considered as the most important item in a balance sheet.

You also need to look into the accounts receivable, short-term investments, and properties, and other liabilities. Take note that the three major categories of a balance sheet are assets, liabilities, and equity.

Assets

All company assets must be categorized under current and noncurrent assets. Assets are considered as current if the company can convert it into cash within 12 months. Net receivables, inventories, and cash are all essential current assets because they are liquid and flexible.

Cash is the top line of the balance sheet. Companies that are generating a lot of cash are usually doing a great job in delivering its products and services to its customers and collecting payments.

High topline can be worrisome, but the low top line is a sign that due diligence should be conducted. But there are companies that don't need a lot of cash to operate. Instead, they choose to reinvest the cash back into the business to improve its profit potential or issue dividends.

Liabilities

Similar to assets, liabilities are also categorized as current or noncurrent. Current liabilities are payables that should be settled within 12 months. In looking for stocks to buy, you should look for companies who have fewer liabilities, especially if compared against the company's cash flow. *Stay away from stocks of companies who owe more money than they bring in.*

The usual liabilities are deferred income, customer deposits, long-term debt, and accounts payable. While assets are often immediate and tangible, liabilities are often considered equally as crucial as debts and other forms of liabilities should be settled before booking a profit.

Equity

Equity refers to the assets less the liabilities. This represents how much the shareholders of a company actually have. In assessing a stock, you should take a look at retained earnings and paid-in capital under the equity section.

Paid-in capital represents the initial investment amount paid by stockholders for their holdings. You need to compare this to added paid-in capital to show the equity premium investors paid above the par value.

This is the main reason why equity concerns are among the top reasons when organizational investors and private funding groups are considering a merger or a business purchase.

Retained profits show the amount of profit that the firm is reinvesting or used to pay down its debt instead of distributing to shareholders as dividends.

Majority of the information you need to assess the debt of a company could be retrieved from the balance sheet. However, some debt obligations and assets are not disclosed there.

Some companies usually possess hard-to-measure intangible assets. Corporate intellectual property such as business processes, copyrights, trademarks, and patents are considered as assets today. However, these are not listed on the balance sheet of the company.

The Volume of Company's Debt and Sales Performance

If you want to invest in stocks, you should look at different financial records to check if this is a worthwhile investment. One of the most important financial metrics that you should scrutinize is the company's debt volume.

It is crucial to learn how you can assess if the debt will affect your dividend investment. But first, we need to take a look at the different forms of debt that a company usually takes.

A company can usually borrow money through two primary methods:

By taking out debt from a bank or other lending organizations such as credit cooperatives
Issuance of fixed-income debt securities such as corporate papers, bills, notes, and bonds.

Most companies are borrowing money from banks, which usually extend credit lines. Established companies usually have open credit lines from which they can draw funds to meet their cash requirement for their daily operations.

The loan that a company takes on from a bank can be used to buy new equipment, purchase additional inventory, or pay company payrolls. More often than not, loans require repayment in a shorter time period compared to most fixed-income securities.

On the other hand, fixed-income securities refer to debt securities that are issued by the company and purchased by investors. If you purchase any form of a fixed-income security, you are basically lending money to a government or business.

In issuing these securities, the company is required to pay underwriting fees. But debt securities allow the company to raise more funds and to borrow for a longer duration compared to the usual terms.

How to Evaluate Company's Debt Volume

As a dividend investor, you should look for a few critical metrics in making your decision whether you want to continue your investment in a company that is about to take on a new debt. Below are some of the important questions you need to ask:

1. How much is the current debt volume of the company?

If a company has zero debt volume, then taking on some loans can actually be beneficial because it can provide the company with more flexibility to reinvest its funds into its operations.

However, if the company you are evaluating already has substantial debt volume, then you may need to dig deeper. In general, high debt volume is not a good sign because it can prohibit the company's ability in creating cash surplus.

Moreover, high debt levels could negatively affect common shareholders who are usually the least priority to be paid when the company goes down.

2. What type of debt is the company taking on?

It is important to take note that loans and fixed-income securities that a company issues have significant differences when it comes to their maturity dates. Some types of loans should be paid within several days after issuance, while others come with longer payment periods.

Usually, debt securities that are issued to the public will have longer maturities compared to the loans offered by private institutions such as banks and large credit organizations.

Long-term fixed-income securities usually have high-interest rates and so may be difficult for the company to pay. But companies may find it hard to repay large short-term loans.

It is crucial for you to assess if the interest rate and length of the debt are suitable for funding the project that the company wants to undertake.

3. What is the purpose of the debt?

Another important factor to consider is the main reason why the company wants to take loans. Is this for a new project or venture with high potential for capital appreciation? Or the company needs to raise money to refinance or repay outstanding debts?

You need to carefully assess this area *before buying stocks in companies that have records of regular debt refinancing.* This signifies that the company doesn't have the ability to meet its financial obligations.

Companies that constantly refinance usually do so because their expenses are higher compared to their revenues. This is not a good sign if you are looking for dividend investments.

But in some special circumstances, it is a good idea for companies to refinance their debt to effectively lower their interest rates. In this case, the debt can reduce the debt volume, which should not be considered as new debt.

4. Can the company afford to pay the debt?

Most established companies are already sure of their ideas before they allocate funds for their execution. However, not all companies are guaranteed with success.

As an investor, it is crucial for you to ascertain whether the company *can still meet its repayments if the project fails.* You should check the cash flow of the company and make sure that it is sufficient to meet its financial obligations. It is best to look for companies that have diversified its prospects.

5. Are there additional provisions that may require sudden demand for repayments?

In assessing the debt volume of a company, you need to check if any special provisions could be damaging once implemented. For instance, there are banks that set a threshold ratio levels. Hence, if any of the company's ratio falls down this threshold, the bank has the right to demand immediate repayment of the loan.

A sudden demand for the company to make payment can magnify any problem inside the company and there are instances where this can lead to liquidation.

Important Financial Ratios for Industry Debt Comparison

Many financial ratios can help you in comparing the debt volume of a company against the industry. Below are the important ratios that you can use:

1. Debt-to-Equity Ratio

This ratio measures the financial leverage of the company. You can get this ratio by dividing long-term debt by the shareholder equity. This signifies what proportions of equity and debt that the company is using to fund its assets.

2. Current Ratio

This ratio in fundamental analysis shows the number of short-term assets versus short-term liabilities. The higher the short-term assets compared to liabilities, the better its capacity to pay off its short-term debt.

3. Acid Test (Quick Ratio)

This ratio will show you the capacity of the company to pay off its short-term debt without the need to sell any inventory.

Remember, a company that is increasing its debt volume must have a plan for repayment. If you have to assess the debt of the company, you need to make certain that the company is aware how the debt can affect its investors, how the debt will be paid, and how long will it take to repay the loan.

Company Sales Performance

Aside from the debt volume, you also need to assess the sales performance of the company you want to buy stocks from. In order to do this, you need to take a look into the price-to-sales ratio, which will allow you to see how the company is using its market capitalization and revenue to figure out whether the stock is worth your money.

To determine the price-to-sales ratio, you need to take the company's market capitalization and divide this by the total sales or revenue of the company over the past 12 months. More often than not, lower price-to-sales ratio signifies a good stock investment.

This metric will help you in determining the value of stocks because it will allow you to see how much the market values every dollar of sales. This ratio is ideal to use if you want to see the value of growth stocks that have yet to be converted into profit.

For instance, if you are looking into a company that is not earning any profit yet, you can take a look at the P/S ratio to figure out if the stock is overvalued or undervalued.

When the P/S ratio is lower compared to other companies in the same sector that is profitable, you may consider purchasing the stock because of low valuation. But be sure also to check other metrics and financial ratios so you can be sure that the stock is properly valued.

With highly cyclical sectors such as airlines, there are some years when only a few companies are producing profits. This doesn't mean that the airline industry is of less value. In such case, investors can use P/S ratio rather than P/E ratio (earnings) in determining how much they are paying for a dollar of their sales instead of their earnings.

When the earnings of the company are negative, the ratio can be considered as not optimal because its capacity will be limited to value the stock because the denominator will be lower than zero.

You can use the P/S ratio for verifying that the growth of a company has not become overvalued or for evaluating recovery scenarios. This will help you in assessing companies that started to suffer losses and has no earnings.

You need to consider how we assess a company that has not made any earnings in the previous 12 months. Unless the company is closing shop, the P/S can be used to determine if the company shares are valued at a discount against others in the same industry.

Let's say that the firm has a P/S of 0.6 while other companies in the sector have a P/S of 2.0. If the company becomes successful in reviving its cash flow, its shares will experience a significant rise as the ratio will become closely matched with other companies in the industry.

On the other hand, companies that are going into negative earnings could also lose the dividend yield. In such case, P/S could signify one of the last remaining metrics for business valuation. A very high P/S can be a red flag while a low P/S can be a good sign.

But you need to take note that turnover is only valuable if you can convert it into earnings. For example, property development firms have high sales turnover but usually takes modest profits.

Meanwhile, a tech company can easily generate $5 in net profit for every $12 in sales revenue. This discrepancy shows that sales dollars cannot always be considered in the same way for each company.

Some investors perceive sales revenue as a more dependable sign of a company's growth. Even though earnings are not always a good indicator of financial wealth, sales revenue metrics are not always reliable.

Evaluating sales performance should be done with a careful assessment of profit margins and compare the findings with other companies within the same sector.

Role of Debt in P/S Ratio Assessment

You should take note that the P/S ratio does not account for the debt on the balance sheet of the company. A company with no debt and a low P/S ratio is a better investment compared to a company with high debt and the same level of P/S.

At this point, the debt can be paid off and the debt will have an interest expense that is associated with it. The P/S ratio as a method of valuation doesn't consider the fact that firms with high debt levels will eventually require higher sales to pay the debt.

However, companies that are on the brink of insolvency and have high debt can rise with low P/S. This can happen if their sales have not experienced a fall while their share price and capitalization breaks down.

So how can you make a better assessment? Some investors are using a method that is effective in figuring out the difference between less healthy, high-debt companies and cheap firms.

You can use the enterprise/value instead of market capitalization/sales. This metric involves the long-term debt of the company. In adding this figure to the company's market capitalization and subtracting any cash on hand, you can determine the enterprise value of the company. The enterprise value is then considered as the total cost of buying the company including the debt and leftover cash.

Like in the case of all valuation techniques, sales-based metrics are only a small part of the assessment. You must consider several metrics to properly value a company. Low P/S could signify unrecognized potential in value as long as other criteria are in places such as high growth prospects, low debt levels, and high-profit margins. Otherwise, using the P/S ratio may result in false value assessment.

Current Dividend Tax Laws

According to the American Shareholders Association, the number of companies distributing dividends to their stockholders had been falling for a quarter of a century before 2003.

This significantly changed after the passage of the Jobs and Growth Tax Relief Reconciliation Act of 2003 (JGTRRA). Alongside other tax reforms introduced to help the economy, the JGTRRA decreased the rate of individual income tax on corporate dividends to 15% and also decreased the rate of the top individual income tax rate on long-term capital gains to 15%.

But this piece of legislation has a sunset provision, and this already expired on 2011. As an investor, you need to take a look at current tax dividend laws to determine how much you need to pay in receiving income from your stock dividends.

JGTRRA had a critical role in the current tax dividend laws as well as ongoing changes. After this passage, around 240 companies had increased the volume of their dividend payouts. This trend continued to rise from 2004 to 2007. This rising trend abruptly ended with the credit crisis and mortgage meltdown in 2008.

Important Provisions of the JGTRRA

The changes in the dividend tax rates caused by the JGTRRA were applied to dividends from "qualifying foreign corporations" and domestic corporations. This involves companies that are incorporated in a country where specific treaties with the US are applicable, companies that are incorporated in a US possession, or US securities exchange.

However, the changes in dividend tax rates do not apply to dividend payouts of the following companies:
- Securities owned through employee stock ownership arrangement
- Companies that are exempted from paying federal income tax
- Stocks owned for fewer than 60 days during the 120 days before and after the announcement of stocks for ex-dividend date.
- Short sale investments that require a related payment in substantially similar or related property
- Real estate investment trusts (REITs)
- Tax-exempt cemetery companies, farmer's cooperatives, mutual savings banks, mutual insurance companies, and credit unions.

Brief Background of Dividend Taxation in the US

To better understand the effect of the JGTRRA, let's go through a short overview of dividend taxation before it took effect in the US.

Basically, taxation started with an initial corporate income tax, at a rate of 35% that was levied against every dollar of the profit that a company earned. After paying this tax, the company may choose to distribute dividends to shareholders. At this point, the payout was considered as income of shareholders and so should be taxed again. For the highest tax bracket of taxpayers, the income tax could reach as high as 39% from every dollar of profit they receive from dividend payouts.

Companies have long expressed their concerns about this double taxation. Remember, the primary objective of corporations is to increase the shareholder value. If companies generate revenue, there are limited number of ways for these profits to be issued to shareholders or reinvested back to business.

Because dividend payouts are considered as inefficient use of capital, companies originally prefer to invest in activities that can generate capital gains, on which investors also paid tax, although at the remarkably reduced rate of 20 per cent.

This encouraged corporations to spend their profits on stock buyback programs, new equipment, acquisitions, research and development, and other activities that can help them build and strengthen their operations. Ideally, these efforts could boost the share price of the company and ultimately could lead to a bigger ROI if investors choose to sell their shares.

This situation significantly changed after the passage of JGTRRA. The decrease of dividend tax rates was one crucial development. Another major change was the decrease in tax on long-term capital gains from 20% to 15% for taxpayers in the highest tax brackets.

JGTRRA equalized the field between different forms of revenue distribution available for companies that are publicly trading.

Advantages of JGTRRA to Investors

Looking for stable dividend payouts from established companies such as Coca-Cola, Johnson & Johnson, and General Electric has been a proven strategy for investors who are looking for steady income.

Investment analysts consider steady dividend payouts as an indicator of strength while stopping dividends is seen as an indicator of weakness. Hence, companies with a strong record of dividend payments have the tendency to keep those payments in the long run.

Established yet slow-growing companies are called widow-orphan stocks because they offer a high degree of safety for investors who are risk averse.

Through JGTRRA, companies that are issuing dividends have become even more enticing for investors, especially for those in the highest tax brackets.

In general, the 15 per cent tax rate on dividends is a good bargain considering the income generated by bonds and other fixed-income securities are taxed at rates of up to 28 per cent.

Investors in the lower tax brackets also take advantage of lower tax rates on dividends with the dividend tax rates falling to only 5 per cent for investors in the 15 per cent or 10 per cent tax categories.

Even though lower taxes are direct and immediate benefits, these are not the only advantage for investors. Just consider the effect on share prices if a firm declares a new dividend payout or approves the increase of their current dividend payout. With these announcements, the share price of the company will become more enticing for investors, and so, the stock prices are more likely to increase. This trend could result in bigger capital gains for investors when they sell their shares.

Aside from the financial benefits, dividend payouts also have advantages in the market psychology. Even though we cannot measure this in a monetary perspective, the increase in the number of companies that are issuing dividends could serve to calm the nerves of the investors in a time of financial crisis.

Advantages of JGTRRA to Corporations

From a corporate perspective, dividends are part of the cost of capital of a company. Decreasing the tax on dividends make it less expensive for companies to do business by making it more affordable for them to give back money to shareholders.

This can also encourage them to invest company profits more efficiently seeking the most profitable business opportunities as opposed to looking for an opportunity that can allow them to avoid issuing dividends.

Company executives gained a lot of benefits from the passage of JGTRRA. Majority of business executives received substantial rewards because they basically rank among the biggest stockholders in the companies that they are running.

Although they do not gain a lot of publicity, corporate executives received massive dividend payouts. Many executives received millions of dollars of dividend payouts. But with the JGTRRA they only had to pay 15% tax as opposed to the 28% tax rate that they would have paid without the legislation.

Even though JGTRRA already ended in 2010, the US Congress has approved the extension of certain provisions until 2012. As an investor, you should be cautious not to put your investments in a position where you will just rely on an income stream that could be substantially reduced.

Interesting Fact #4

Ticker Tapes: Before you could trade stocks online or see which stocks and securities were trading in real time on TV, your computer or mobile phone, brokers relied on stock ticker tapes, which printed out stock price information that was transmitted over telegraph lines. The ticking sound as the paper printed is how it earned its name.

Chapter 4

High Dividend Yield Strategy

In dividend stock investing, many investors are following the high dividend yield strategy. This particular strategy could result in large cash income, usually from slow-growth companies that have a substantial cash volume to finance dividend payouts.

However, the unnecessary focus on income alone often obscures the important reality that long-term stock dividend investment is based on the total return of a portfolio, which includes both capital and income growth.

This scenario raises two important questions:

1. How does its total-return performance compare to the profits of other potential stock-option strategies?
2. With a focus on income, how has the total profit of a high-dividend yield strategy fared in comparison to the overall market?

Take note that a high-dividend yield strategy is a systematic approach in buying and holding stocks wherein the dividend is high relative to the share price. As such, this is a strategy that prefers stock valuation because this it's actually the low price of the stock in relation to the dividend, which mainly causes the high yield.

But a high-dividend yield strategy is just one form of strategy in dividend investing, which can help you in selecting stocks. There is also considerable proof and theoretical foundation that value stocks can outperform both market and growth stocks in the long run. In this perspective, the "yield" premium that is linked to high-dividend strategies really refers to the value premium.

Other strategies focus on stocks based on high earnings or high cash flow relevant to price as well as the high book value of equity that is relevant to market value.

One possible explanation for the minimal return of the high-dividend yield stocks compared to stocks chosen via other value metrics is that dividend stocks are usually sourced from bigger companies.

Companies that are not issuing dividends are not included in the list. Therefore, a high-dividend yield strategy foregoes to a higher degree the available return premium available from investing in smaller companies.

Stocks that are chosen on the basis of high profits often demonstrate strong performance. This value strategy could purchase non-dividend-payment of growth companies that are not included in the list and also companies that are generating enough revenues but have reduced their dividend payouts or they are temporarily suspended.

It is important to take note that no single value strategy could outperform consistently over shorter time frames. Therefore, the diversifying strategy can be beneficial at this point, especially for investors who are a bit impatient.

One major advantage of choosing high-dividend stocks is that they are less volatile in the market. But value stocks based on either cash flow or earnings had modestly higher risk-adjusted profits compared to high-dividend yield strategy.

A high-dividend strategy could result in less stock turnover compared to a strategy that is based on earnings or cash flow and in this case, it can drastically lower capital gains taxes.

But a strategy that is based on high book-to-market can also decrease turnover and potential capital gains taxes. In general, with a focus on consistent and significant taxable income generation, a high-dividend strategy is not tax efficient, especially in countries with higher dividend tax rates compared to the US.

Remember, a high-dividend yield strategy has several advantages for dividend investors. This is easy to understand and usually attractive to the innate desire of investors to hold on to their shares. Stocks selected using high-dividend yield strategy are often powerful enough to outperform the market with less volatility.

But if we base this on absolutes, its returns have affected other value strategies. Using the risk-adjusted perspective, the lower volatility can come at a cost of lower returns.

High-dividend yield strategy may not be applicable to wealthy investors or high-income earners. This strategy could trigger unnecessary income that created unnecessary tax drag on the accumulation of wealth.

In summary, investors, especially those that are subject to taxes, might be better off creating a cash flow stream using a systematic withdrawal program from an investment portfolio that attracts higher returns from other values strategies instead of depending solely on a high-dividend yield strategy.

The Advantages of Selecting High-Dividend Yield Stocks

Majority of dividend-paying stocks are in defensive sectors that are poised to sustain economic crises with less volatility. More often than not, dividend-paying companies have significant amounts of cash. Hence, these are established companies with better prospects in the long-term.

Dividend Yields as Regular Cash Stream

Bear in mind that the dividend yield is a financial metric that will help you figure out how much per share a company is paying out per annum in the dividend. This is expressed in percentage.

As a review, you can calculate the dividend yield by taking the yearly dividend per share divided by the price for each share. This will provide a percentage as the dividend yield, as the majority of companies are issuing dividends every quarter.

Dividends can provide a regular source of income for stock investors. You can use this passive revenue to spend or reinvest back in stocks. This is a common practice in the industry.

Investors who are about to retire or are already in retirement usually choose dividend stocks as a source of revenue as long as these stocks are less volatile.

Dividend-paying stocks will allow you to make money in two methods:
- Stock price appreciation
- Distributions issued by the company

Majority of the companies that are issuing stocks have dividend reinvestment plans, which allow investors to use dividends in purchasing more shares in the company.

This will allow you to gradually build a bigger position in a company in the long run. Many companies are not taking commissions for these added shares. Some are even offering discounts.

Companies are offering reinvestment plans because they take advantage of having a base of long-term investors who are actively involved in the future of the business.

Dividend Stocks Are Based in Defensive Sectors

Majority of the companies that are paying dividends are in defensive industries, which are seen as non-cyclical. These companies are not dependent on bigger economic cycles.

Defensive stocks can withstand economic instability and they are generally less volatile compared to the overall market. This can be a great thing for investors who are risk-averse. These stocks can pay more than investors can receive from conservative securities such as bonds. Hence they are great additions to investment portfolios.

Typical defensive sectors include healthcare, pharmaceutical, utility and housing, and food industries. Even during financial uncertainty, people still need to buy food products and keep the lights on.

Regardless of the status of the economy, people still get sick and require medical care. Healthcare stocks such as Pfizer are usual favorites of investors who love high-dividend stocks.

Established Companies

Majority of companies that are paying dividends are already established companies with well-performing stocks. They have the capacity to distribute dividends to investors because they have a substantial cash reserve. For this reason, they are good stocks to include in your portfolio. Examples of such companies are Coca-Cola and Procter & Gamble that pay 3.5% and 3.95% dividends per year.

In the long run, established companies perform better. Based on a stock analysis published by Forbes in 2015, dividend-paying stocks have shown better performance since 1927. The average growth of dividend-paying stocks is 10.4% compared to the 8.5% annual growth of non-dividend-paying stocks.

Dividend-paying stocks are also less volatile. The average deviation for dividend-paying stocks is 18% while non dividend-paying stocks are at 30%.

The Downsides of High Yield Dividend Stocks

The primary risks of high yield dividend stocks include interest rate risk and inability to make dividend payments. High yield dividend stocks could be remarkable opportunities for savvy investors who can earn a substantial amount from their investments while waiting for the prospect of stock appreciation. Hence, it is crucial to perform proper and deeper due diligence to make sure that dividend payouts are possible.

Remember, high yield dividend strategy works by choosing stocks that have *strong balance sheets* and managed by a well-experienced and skilled management team. There are instances that companies with great records of issuing payouts encounter short-term problems or poor market conditions that cause temporary hiccups. This can temporarily raise the dividend yield, which creates opportunities for savvy investors.

Remember, stocks are often affected by the performance of the underlying business as well as the interest rates. If interest rates increase, dividends could become less attractive to investors, which result in equity outflows and selling of stocks.

Many high dividend stocks are in consumer staples, master limited partnerships, utilities, and real estate investment trusts (REITs). Huge cap indexes such as S&P 100 and Dow Jones also contain a lot of high dividend stocks.

High Dividend as an Indicator of Company Distress

Although high dividends are typically attractive to investors, some are actually considered as fool's gold. In some instances, a high dividend may indicate that a company is experiencing distress. You may lose your investment during dividend cuts or stock price falls if you only choose stocks solely on the basis of the dividend.

The stock market is a forward-looking market and usually doesn't account for the underlying problems of a company. This can make the dividend more enticing for investors.

Let's say that CGF Inc is trading at $50 and issues $2.50 yearly dividend. Hence, we have a 5% dividend yield. Some movement in the market could result in a loss in earnings capacity, and the share price of the company falls to $25. This is a 50% loss. In the case of dividends, they are not automatically ceased. Hence, on the surface, some investors may see that the yield on CGF stock is now at 10 per cent.

But this high dividend yield is only temporary as the same factors that caused the fall of the share price would most likely lead to a decrease in a dividend. In other scenarios, the company may choose to keep the dividend to reward loyal stockholders. Hence, you should not ignore the need to look into the operations and the financials of the company. This will help you determine if the dividend payouts are sustainable.

Some important factors to scrutinize are the status of the company's overall financial health, management's strategy, increases and decreases, historical dividend schedules, historical payout ratio, and free cash flow.

Many of the best dividend paying companies are usually blue chips in the sector with a stable record of generating revenue and income growth over several quarters and years. This reputation and credibility usually lend itself to the stable underlying fundamentals that are associated with most companies that are paying dividends.

With this, there will always be new players entering into the mix and companies who are starting to struggle with their dividend payout. Hence, it is crucial to maintain steadfast due diligence.

Risk of Interest Rate

Dividend yields are often being compared to the risk-free rate of return that typically increases in scenarios where the government is implementing stricter financial policies.

As a result, many investors assess dividend and dividend investments in relation to this metric instead of absolute basis. If the interest rates increase, it could lead to outflows in high dividend yield stocks and may also cause stock prices to decrease. Significant changes in interest rates could be a catalyst for some market movements and possibly result in a bear market. Hence, this is a crucial factor to follow for different investing decisions.

The US government has been increasing interest rates since 2015. The stricter policy is affecting the nearly a decade of bullish returns of the stock market. This has also been aligned with increasing inflation, improving the economy and recovery of the labor market.

The year 2019 may be a good time to consider some of the best high dividend stocks and reallocate some investments. This will allow you to take advantage of a higher risk-free rate in liquid cash savings as well as short-term bonds.

Interesting Fact #5

Opening Bell: Since 1903, the start of every day's trading session on the NYSE starts with the ringing of an actual bell at 9:30 a.m. Eastern Standard Time. Originally, the signal was a gavel, and then a gong. Many high-profile people have been invited to participate in the tradition of ringing the opening bell, including singer Usher, former President Ronald Reagan, actor Robert Downey, Jr., firefighters and Star Wars villain Darth Vader.

Chapter 5

High Dividend Growth Rate Strategy

High dividend growth rate strategy requires buying of stocks in companies that are presently paying lower-than-average dividends but are growing so rapidly that within 5 to 10 years, the absolute dollar amounts collected from the equity could be higher than what you can receive using the high dividend yield strategy.

Even though companies that are paying high dividends have performed remarkably well in recent years, they have become a bit expensive in terms of most valuation metrics. While they can still pay high dividends, the previous low-interest rate setting pushed many of these companies to get more into debt to expand their reach. When interest rates increased, many of these companies are now under pressure.

On the other hand, stocks with a track record of dividend growth can present a compelling investment opportunity in a setting of rising rates and potential volatility. Investing in companies with growing and sustainable dividends will provide you the opportunity to hold high-quality stocks and higher income over time. To some extent, this will allow you to buffer against market volatility and address the risk of increasing rates.

This strategy goes beyond the conventional realm of domestic large-cap stocks. This is also effective for small and medium stocks and can also be applied to global stock markets.

Why Choose Dividend Growers?

Basically, quality dividend growth stocks tend to be of higher quality compared to those in the wider market when it comes to leverage and earnings quality. In most cases, if a company is capable of boosting its dividend payout for years, this is a good indicator that it has discipline and financial strength.

Be that as it may, the high dividend yield does not always guarantee that the company is well-disciplined or has financial strength. There are instances when new or struggling companies tried to entice market investors by taking on more debt just to issue higher dividends.

Because of this, high-dividend payers with lower earnings growth, lower profitability, and higher financial leverage are more likely to cut down their dividends during a low-growth and volatile market.

Buffer Against Market Volatility

High dividend growth stocks can be enticing to investors who are looking for established companies that can withstand stressful market and economic settings. Specifically, dividend growth stocks may provide some disadvantage during bearish markets.

Increasing Rates Risk

High dividend growth stocks can easily address the concerns surrounding the performance of high dividend payers when the rates increase in the market.

Because of its concentration on increasing dividends instead of high yield, the performance of dividend growers is less powered by the value factor in comparison with the high dividend payers. As the stock market shifts toward growth, the performance of high growth stocks is less likely to suffer.

Not similar to many pure yield strategies that tend to be focused on industries such as financials, consumer staples, and utilities, high dividend growth strategy has the tendency to include more diversified industries. Hence, the industry composition of this strategy is more stable in the long run. Diversification can help during major movements in the performance of specific sectors.

Given the concentration on quality balance sheets, a high dividend growth can be ideal to investors who are worried about volatility and the possibility of increasing rates but still prefer to hold stocks that will generate them income. If you prefer this arrangement, a high dividend growth strategy is recommended for you.

According to hypothetical analysis, dividend growth stocks can easily generate more revenue over time compared to stocks with a higher yield but with slower growth of dividend.

Although the yield on a growth-oriented stocks is initially lower compared to yield-oriented stocks, an increasing dividend and an increasing share price could lead to a more stable long-term total return.

Choosing the Largest Stream of Net Present Value Dividends

Let's say you need to choose between two different dividend-paying stocks. Which would you include in your portfolio?

- Company A has a dividend yield of 3.5%. The company has a track record of increasing the dividend by 5% per year and the current dividend payout ratio is at 60 per cent.
- Company B has a dividend yield of 0.80%. It is growing at a fast rate of 20%. The current dividend payout ratio is 10 per cent.

With everything else equal, you are more likely to choose Company B if you are following a high dividend growth rate strategy. Company A may look like the better choice, but if you choose Company B, you will end up cashing in bigger aggregate dividend checks when you own stocks from Company B, as long as the growth could be sustained in the next decade.

As the dividends increase alongside earnings, the yield-on-cost begins to overtake the company with minimal growth.

Eventually, the core business will reach its full potential and majority of the surplus generated every year will support reinvestment plus dividend payout. When this milestone is achieved, stockholder-friendly business management will return the excess profits to the owners through share buybacks or dividend payouts.

Good examples are Wal-Mart and McDonald's. During the early years of their business, when these companies were conquering each state in the US, the dividends were not very high. But investors who had bought their stocks were able to collect a fairly huge dividend yield on their cost basis within five to eight years.

Investors in the 1970s and the 1980s who used the high dividend growth strategy would not miss these present-day blue chip stocks.

Growth Is an Indicator of a Healthy Business

Which scenario will give you peace of mind?

- Owning stocks of a company that is paying you huge dividend today and is seeing a slow decline in its core business
- Owning stocks of a company that is paying you a smaller dividend today but enjoys higher profits each year

If you think there is a level of extra security in the company, you may want to consider a high dividend growth strategy. This is a wiser approach.

The board of directors of a company is unlikely to increase the dividend if they think they are going to have to cut it soon. Hence, a rising dividend rate on a per share basis usually signifies a vote of confidence from the people who have seen and analyzed the company's balance sheet and income statement.

But take note that this is not foolproof. Business executives who have the skills and expertise to serve in the board of directors are still vulnerable to self-deception, especially if it falls down to their own interest. But more often than not, this is a good indicator of company health.

Financial Gravity and Dividend Growth Investing

The biggest risk to the high dividend growth rate strategy is a primary macro movement that is beyond your control as an investor. This is the rate of interest in the market.

In fact, Warren Buffet calls interest rates as the financial gravity, because it seems universal in the financial world. All financial assets that will pay you some form of income streams such as interest income, dividends, and earnings are all priced relative to the interest rates determined by the government.

In comparison to historic standards, the stock PEs today are near nose-bleed levels while the dividends are minimal. This is primarily due to the current situation where the US Federal Reserve has pushed down the yield on all federal bonds to remarkably low levels.

Basically, the short-term federal bonds are considered as representative of the risk-free interest rate that you can earn on your money. Hence, all other assets are priced relative to these bonds. If the federal bond yields plummet, many investors look for instruments that can provide higher yields such as stocks.

This has been beneficial for investors over the two decades. As the interest rates fall the share price and bonds have increased, keeping the bond and stock markets floating and even generating enough capital gains.

It becomes problematic when interest rates start to increase - as they will do eventually. While the long term trend gravitates towards lower dividend yield, the interest rates still follow a cycle. They still rise and fall to keep the inflation in check and aids in boosting the economy. With interest rates at an all-time low, there's no way to go but up.

As an example, let's take a closer look at a hypothetical federal 30 year bond that yields 2% per annum and a hypothetical company known as Riveratic with stock at $100. Let's also say that similar to federal bonds, Riveratic's profits are not growing. Meanwhile, the financial position of the company is quite solid so its stock yield stands at 4 per cent.

In making an investment decision, you need to tackle this tradeoff. If you need a higher yield, you would definitely buy stocks of Riveratic. But if you need a rock solid stream of interest payouts you would definitely choose the federal bonds.

What will happen if the yield of the federal bond increases to 4%? In this case, both the Riveratic stocks and the 30 year federal bonds will yield the same amount. Now, which would you rather invest in?

Considering the same growth rate and the higher risk in Riveratic profits, you would go for federal bonds. In this case, there is no actual benefit in investing in Riveratic stocks. However, there is significant downside risk.

Other dividend investors will see this, so if the government rates increase, investors are willing to pay less for stocks or non-federal bonds. Share prices will fall to correct the relative valuation. In this case, Riveratic's dividend yield would have to double to recover its proper valuation versus federal bonds.

As a result, the share price would be decreased by 50%. Those who invested in Riveratic stocks would have lost the same percentage of their capital. And this will not be a short-term loss. That money will not be recovered.

Federal bonds today yield at 2.35% and the dividend growth stocks are not providing higher yield. Once US government rates eventually increase, investors who have invested in stocks priced on yield or profits will also lose a lot of money.

Dividend Growth Rate Strategy Is not a Fail-Proof Strategy

Majority of growth-oriented companies have increased their share prices as investors look forward to a long string of growing dividend payouts. But there is still a risk if the company fails to deliver its promises, which is fairly common in the business world.

Many businesses, even those that are already established ones, are managed by a business executive who is still prone to commit errors. For example, Best Buy was one of the most promising growth-oriented company for many years.

Looking back at its track record, it was easy to see a remarkable record of profit and growth. The company had a stable balance sheet and was even buying back shares. This stock price increased to reflect the past record of the company. However, in 2006, there was a clear indicator that the Best Buy's stock performance is no longer sustainable.

The company's growth started to slow down and its solid performance shifted into losses. The stock plummeted from $60 in 2006 to just $12 in 2012. Shareholders lost around 80 per cent of their holdings and the Best Buy stock is yet to fully recover from its loss (as of Feb 2019).

Unfortunately, this is not an isolated case. Companies experience major declines in performance. According to research conducted by Richard Foster from Yale University, the average lifespan of a company included in the S&P 500 plummeted from 67 years in the 1920s to just 15 years in 2015.

One of the primary reasons companies are eliminated from the index is due to financial distress. In fact, in 2015, around 44 companies in the S&P Index paid more than 100 per cent of their EPS!

Stock analysts today agree that dividend growth over the years will slow down by 45 per cent. This is an early indicator of financial distress.

Moreover, there are many companies that are no longer investing in profit-generating assets. The common practice nowadays is to use cash flow to decrease shareholder equity. This could pump up reported profits, but eventually, even this strategy has its own limitations. The share price traction of companies that are cutting dividends is usually not good.

Dividend growth investing precludes strong margins of safety, which would help in protecting against performance decline. The primary focus of this strategy is on growth and not on safeguarding principle that demands a strong safety margin.

Remember, there is a limit on dividend growth, and by paying up for assumed growth, you might be putting your capital at serious risk in the prospect of increasing your passive income.

Stock Performance of Growth-Oriented Dividend Stocks

If you like to hold a decent stream of growing dividends, then you need to choose companies with strong competitive advantages. This is one of the strategies used by Warren Buffett.

Without this, the company performance is likely to go back to a more usual level of growth and profitability and the value of your stock is likely to crater as a result.

This is known as reversion to the mean and it is a common phenomenon in the financial world.

Competitive advantages (also referred to as moats by Buffet) will gradually weaken over time. Remember, moats cannot protect your castle forever. Time will come that new technology will be developed and disrupt the core business.

But let's say that you really want to focus on looking for firms with solid moats. Companies such as Google, Harley Davidson, and Coca Cola are some of the obvious ones. However, these companies are expensive today.

There is always the possibility that your gut feeling is wrong. In addition, many investors under-estimate the skills and experience needed to execute a high dividend growth rate strategy.

The dividend growth stocks that are performing well today are considered as the survivors. These are the companies that have been consistent and withstood the test of time, while other companies in the same sector already closed shop or are still struggling.

Bear in mind that the survival of a dividend growing company over a number of years could either be driven by its competitive advantage or luck. The company's previous performance has no effect on its present business.

Interesting Fact #6

Blue Chips: This prestigious nickname is reserved for companies that are nationally known and trade high on the stock market. The name is derived from the highest value poker chip, which is blue. Companies considered "blue chips" include General Mills, the Kellogg Company, IBM and Johnson & Johnson.

Chapter 6

How to Find the Best Quality Dividend Stocks for Your Portfolio

At this point, you should already understand that dividend investing is a slow and steady way of stock market investing. But this method can help you eventually win the race. Warren Buffett, the Oracle of Omaha, is popular for investing in blue-chip stocks that are paying dividends.

Dividend investing has helped Buffet to become one of the richest men on Earth. He is also popular for his strategy of reinvesting dividends. This approach is an effective tactic in stock market investing. Dividends will provide you protection from inflation, which is non-existent when it comes to bonds.

At first, this strategy may seem very easy to follow. After all, you have to look for companies that are paying dividends. Then instead of cashing out those dividends, you can reinvest them so you can gradually build your wealth.

Unfortunately, it's not that easy. You should make certain that you are investing your money in a company that has good traction and prospects. Ignoring due diligence could lead to a depreciation of share price, elimination of dividend, or dividend cuts.

In this Chapter, we will discuss the important factors that you should look for in a stock dividend:

Low Earnings, Strong Cash Projections

Consistent cash flow should be your number one criteria in choosing stock dividends for your portfolio. Stay away from companies that are not consistently profitable.

It is easy to see healthy dividend returns from companies that can deliver you profits but not profitable growth on a yearly basis. But because there are companies that are growing as well as consistently making profits, it is nonsense to select the former. Be strict in your criteria and only choose companies that demonstrate growth and profitability.

Ideally, you should look for long-term profit growth expectations between 5 percent and 15 per cent. You should not go beyond 15 per cent because of the high probability of revenue disappointments that may affect the share price.

Even though profits can drive profitable growth and are an important indicator of a quality dividend-paying business, you should always take note that dividends will be sourced out from the company cash flow. In this case, the next step is to ensure that the company has the capacity to generate cash sustainably (i.e. the company is not in a very cyclical industry, the company has shown to either maintain or improve their margins etc.)

You should also look for companies that have increased their dividend payouts in the last five years. This significantly increases the odds of sustainable dividend growth, which is a huge plus for investors. And of course, you need to buy the shares before the ex-dividend date.

Check Sector Health

Most investors often overlook the importance of checking the health of the industry. At this moment, the banking industry is suffering because of additional regulation and the emergence of disruptive technology. The share prices have sold off, and because of weakening demand, share price appreciation and dividend increases may not happen in the future.

Meanwhile, with an ageing population, the demand for care services for the old will increase in the next 20 to 30 years. This doesn't guarantee that stocks of healthcare companies will be immune to wider market plunges, but they are more likely to become more resilient compared to other stocks. There is a higher chance of dividend appreciation as long as the industry is doing well.

The point here is that you should never choose a stock based on history because it doesn't guarantee the future. Let's consider the case of carbonated beverages. With the emergence of health consciousness among consumers, investing in soda companies doesn't guarantee success like it used to in the past.

The big players in this industry are now shifting into the alternative drink niche but it will take some time before they can catch up with the demand. Take the smoother road instead of a rough one.

Avoid Companies with High Debt

On your prospect list, eliminate the dividend-paying companies with too much debt. You can learn about the company's current debt situation by looking at its debt-to-equity ratio. Look elsewhere if the company's D/E ratio is high.

However, you may still want to consider excluding stocks with D/E ratio upwards of 2.00. The ideal ratio is 1.00, which will give you peace of mind.

This is actually quite basic. If the company has excessive debt, then it will need to pay its debt at some point. Once the debt becomes due, it will require the extra cash to settle. This may affect dividend payouts.

Be sure to check the company's net debt-to-capital. Although it could be helpful during special circumstances, financial leverage can be quite dangerous. If you have felt the pains of overpriced home mortgage or credit card debt you will understand that borrowed money could be problematic if we overextend ourselves.

The same is true for businesses regardless of size and industry. This is the primary reason why you should take a look at the net debt-to-capital ratio of the company. This financial metric will tell you how much debt the business is using for its operations.

If a business has $100 Million worth of equipment, it acquired this important asset through a combination of equity and debt. You can figure out what percentage of a company's financing is from debt if you take a look at its debt-to-capital ratio.

Let's say that the equipment was supported by 30% debt and 70% equity. The debt-to-capital ratio of the company would appear as follows total book debt ($30 million) divided by total book debt ($30 million) plus equity ($70).

These figures would lead to a debt-to-capital ratio of 30% ($30M / $100M). To put it simply, debt accounts for 30% of the capital structure of the company we are looking at.

It is ideal to invest in a company with a net debt-to-capital ratio that is not higher than 50%. However, some sectors such as utilities could reasonably take on higher debt levels because of the *stability of their revenue.*

When a business suddenly falls during an economic recession and has high debt volume and interest to pay with its limited cash flow, the stock price could be dramatically affected and the dividend payout could become much riskier. Take note that companies will always prioritize their debt obligations before they pay a dividend.

Choose Companies that Offer Real Value

You might be attracted by businesses that are "booming" based on stock price. However, there is always the risk of you chasing the market, which is not always the best move you can make.

It is ideal to consider stocks of companies that are trading below their actual value. Businesses that have products or services that are of high quality and value are more likely to succeed.

While their share price may look average or below average, the value of what they can offer to their customers could usually make certain that their performance becomes more consistent over time.

But even businesses that are seeing a sharp decline in their stock price could be a lucrative choice to add in your portfolio. You should assess every business based on merits. A lower stock price can provide you the opportunity to invest in these companies below their actual value.

At face value, investing in a company whose stock price plummets at an unpredicted market movement may look like a bad decision. However, if you could see that the core business of the company shall continue to stay in demand in the next 20 to 30 years, one small incident will not make the company a bad investment.

As a matter of fact, the best time to buy company stocks is when their stocks are undervalued. As an investor, you should know how to assess the events that could damage the company or the whole industry and evaluate and if depreciating stock prices could reflect the whole value of the product or service that they offer. On the other hand, it may be a good time to buy into them while dividend stocks are trading below their real value.

Choose Companies with Excellent Management

You should pick companies that are managed by business executives that demonstrate discipline and excellence. The company managers play a vital role in creating wealth for you as a stockholder.

At first, it could be a bit difficult to determine if a company has a good management team. But the longer back you go, the more you can see if the business has a robust and consistent track record. Go through their previous financial statements and check how true or false management projections were (i.e. do they tend to exaggerate a lot or simply say the truth).

You should compare the performance of the company in comparison to similar companies in the sector over five years or 10 years. In addition, you should also see how the company has performed in comparison to the market index. If you are confident that the market is working out the truth, then the record should be manifested in the stock price.

Try to figure out which companies have decided to buy back shares when their shares are trading below value. This can help in adding stockholder wealth if the share prices begin to rise as this could reduce the number of shares. This is a good indicator that the management is loyal to their core business.

Meanwhile, you should be wary of businesses that are buying up other businesses beyond their industry or area of expertise. This is usually an indicator that the management is overreaching to grow the company.

Stay Away from Companies with Excessive Dividend Yields

It is ideal to stay away from any company that is offering dividend yields of more than 10% especially if the market average stands at or near 4.5 per cent. This is an indicator that the market believes that the current payout ratio of the company and its dividends are not sustainable.

Take note that the yield is based on historical dividend payouts over the last 12 months as a portion of the existing stock price. Just because a business has a history of maintaining certain dividend yield levels in the past, doesn't mean that they are still capable of doing so in the future. A plummeting stock price could mirror the expectation of the market for lower dividends in the future.

This may also mean that the business is using debt instruments to finance dividend payouts for stockholders. This is known as a dividend recapitalization. It is crucial to look at the cash track record of the company going back several years. This will allow you to avoid companies that are using debt to finance their dividend payouts. By doing this, you can also figure out how much of the dividend has come from the company's own cash profits.

You should bear in mind that if the dividend payouts are constantly lower than the amount of cash flow that the business has, it will help you to assess if they have the capacity to pay the dividend in the future.

Choose Stable Companies

In general, dividend companies are considered more stable because they usually provide basic necessities such as housing, gas, electricity, water, food, and even hygiene products. Hence, the typical sectors for dividends include:

- Real estate
- Finance
- Consumer staples (food, clothing, toiletries)
- Utilities
- Energy
- Telecommunications

Regardless of the state of the economy, people will always buy these products and services. Hence, the companies that provide them are usually more stable. Companies that are less stable usually provide products and services that people can easily let go - travel, restaurants, music, cellphones, and computers.

But every rule has its exceptions. Surely, many financials shattered the norm during the 2007 stock market bubble. However, the warning signs were already visible even before the bubble peaked. Savvy investors who saw the signs and read the "writing on the wall" bailed out early.

But in general, dividend companies are considered more stable compared to non-dividend companies. As a matter of fact, paying dividends is regarded as one key factor that helped some financial companies to survive the crash, assuming they have declined government bail out.

Dividend investors usually think that established companies are paying out a big percentage of their revenue as dividends because there are limited investment options that offer decent returns. But there is a more nuanced view in reality.

One example is the case of General Electric (GE), which is a matured company that has consistently increased its dividend payouts. However, the company has invested a nice percentage of its profits into diversification and growth. It has built and currently runs a dozen primary business units from household appliances to jet aircraft engines.

Interesting Fact #7

The Dutch East India Company, which is involved in the spice trade, was among the first companies to offer shares. Shareholders didn't have much influence – the company was controlled by its directors. However, shareholders were richly rewarded. The annual dividends were 16% on average over the first half of the 17th century.

Chapter 7

Where to Find Information on Companies

Picking stocks to buy for your dividend portfolio requires a lot of time and effort for research and analysis. Also, you need to compete with stock market professionals and fund managers who have more experience and have exclusive access to valuable insights.

But if you have the time and resources to keep an eye on the dividend market and the economy, this will be a worthwhile endeavor as dividends can provide you stable passive income and possible growth of your wealth over time.

Understand the Current US Economy and Financial Environment

It is crucial to take a closer look at the current US economy and financial setting before you start buying dividend stocks. Educate yourself about how the market and economic movements can affect your dividend investments.

You can make better investment decisions if you can access reliable information. Below are the best places where you can read information about market changes:

The Federal Reserve System

The board publishes a regular Financial Stability Report. This report summarizes the framework of the Federal Reserve Board in evaluating the status and resilience of the American financial system. The board also publishes special economic research to help investors gauge specific industries.

The research section of banks and stockbrokers

You should read expert forecasts about economic conditions in the US

Business newspapers such as:

- The Wall Street Journal
- Financial Times
- The Economic Times
- Business Standard
- International Business Times
- Investor's Business Daily

The business section of reputable newspapers such as:

- The New York Times
- Chicago Tribune
- The New York Post
- Los Angeles Times
- The Washington Post
- The Mercury News
- Credible business websites such as:
- Yahoo Finance
- Forbes
- MSN Money Central
- CNN Money
- WSJ
- Google Finance
- Bloomberg
- CNBC

High-quality business magazines such as:

- Forbes
- Bloomberg Businessweek
- WIRED
- Entrepreneur

- Fortune
- Inc
- The Economist
- Consumer Reports

Topics that you should be updated with are the following:

- The American economy
- The US economic policy
- The interest rates
- Exchange rates
- Overseas markets and economies relevant to the industry you want to invest with
- Investor sentiment

You should also get updates on sector-specific or even local influences that could affect business profits.

Finding Dividend Stocks to Buy

1. Blue Chip Companies

If you want to choose your own dividend stocks, a great place, to begin with, is the S&P 500, which is a list of top 500 companies in the USA, popularly known as "blue chip" companies.

These companies are often well-established companies that are ideal for investors who are looking for stable returns with less risk. The top blue-chip companies that are paying dividends in the US are the following:

- American Capital Agency Corp
- Southern Copper Corp
- NuStar Energy L.P.
- AT&T Inc
- STMicroelectronics N.V.

- Lockheed Martin Corp.
- Eli Lilly & Co.
- Paychex Inc
- H&R Block Inc
- United Parcel Service Inc (UPS)

2. Speculative Companies

Businesses that are relatively new in the stock market and are not in the top 100 companies in the US are called speculative companies. While there is always the potential to gain huge returns, you may also suffer heavy losses. Speculative stocks are ideal for well-experienced investors who have the resources to risk their capital to gain higher returns. Also, there are very few speculative companies that are paying dividends.

3. Invest Your Money In a Company / Industry You Know

If you are just getting started in dividend investing, it is ideal to begin with a sector or business that you understand. You will have a much better chance to assess if the business is strong or weak if you are familiar with the sector.

Take note that the US economy and the stock market are categorized into two major tiers. The upper tier (known as a sector) is a wide category of companies that have similar economic qualities. At present, there are 11 major sectors in the US that most dividend investors use in breaking down the companies.

Meanwhile, the sectors are categorized further by industry, which allows a narrower grouping of companies with similar businesses. For instance, luxury jeweler Tiffany & Company, and discount retail chain Dollar Tree are categorized in the consumer discretionary sector but they are categorized into separate industries.

Taking a closer look at industries and sectors will allow you to compare one company to its competitors. There is no way to know for sure if a specific dividend stock is good for purchase unless you assess the current competition.

Looking at industries and sectors will also help you become more familiar with how companies engage with one another. For instance, if you think that energy prices will fall, you may focus your attention on transportation shares because you think that among the largest cost inputs - jet fuel and gasoline - is about to fall. If used with long-term, low-turnover, discipline, and tax-efficient dividend investing, this knowledge can help you amass great wealth.

Stock Market Industry Sector Breakdown

In the US exchange, the stocks market has the following industry sectors:

a) Utilities

This is composed of water, gas, and electric companies including integrated providers. This industry generates stable recurring income by charging businesses and individual homes. Companies under this sector usually provide bigger dividend yields compared to other sectors.

b) Financials

This is composed of real estate firms, insurance companies, investment funds, and banks. Basically, the majority of the profits generated by the industry comes from loans and mortgages that gain value when interest rates increase.

c) Consumer Discretionary

This sector is composed of consumer durables, apparel companies, consumer service providers, media companies, and retailers. Basically, these companies take advantage of an improving economy when customer spending skyrockets.

d) Consumer Staples

The consumer staples sector is composed of food and beverage businesses and other companies that manufacture products that the majority of customers are not willing to forego from their every day living. Basically, companies in the consumer staples sector are capable of surviving and even thriving in a financial downturn.

e) Healthcare

The healthcare sector is composed of medical device manufacturers, hospital management companies, pharmaceuticals, biotechnology firms, and more. This sector is considered as both defensive and growth sector as people will always need healthcare.

f) Energy

The energy sector is composed of energy production companies, oil and gas exploration firms, and integrated power businesses. These companies are generating profits that are tied to the price of natural gas, crude oil, and other commodities.

g) Telecom

The telecom sector is composed of satellite companies, internet service providers, cable companies, and wireless providers. These companies generate recurring revenue from consumers. However, some subcategories of the industry are experiencing rapid changes.

h) Technology

This sector is composed of information technology firms, software developers, and electronics manufacturers. Basically, these businesses are driven by the general health of the economy and upgrade cycles, even though it has experienced growth over the years.

i) Real Estate

The real estate sector is composed of companies that are invested in retail, industrial, and residential real estate. The primary source of profits for this sector comes from real estate capital appreciation and rental income. Hence, this sector is quite vulnerable to changes in the interest rate.

j) Industrial

This sector is composed of manufacturing, fabrication, construction, machinery, defense, and aerospace companies. Basically, the growth in this industry is driven by the demand for manufactured and construction products such as agricultural tools and equipment.

k) Materials

The materials sector is composed of forestry, chemical, refining, and mining-related companies that are mainly focused on discovering and developing raw materials. Because these companies are at the start of the supply chain, these are sensitive to the changes in the business cycle.

When you have a list of companies, it will help you a lot to consider the current competition and how it stands compared to other companies in the sector.

You must figure out:
- The position of the company in the market
- The sustainability of the products and services that the company provides
- The growth opportunity of the company in the future

Company Due Diligence

Remember, the value of your dividend investment depends on the health of the company. Hence, it is crucial to perform the necessary due diligence before you buy shares.

Due diligence refers to an audit or investigation of a possible dividend investment so you can verify all the available facts. This includes the review of all financials on top of other necessary materials.

In the finance world, due diligence is conducted by companies who want to make acquisitions. This could be performed by investment analysts, investment brokers/dealers, fund managers, or equity research analysts.

For individual dividend investors, due diligence is voluntary yet highly recommended. However, investment brokers are legally mandated to perform due diligence before selling. This will prevent them from being held liable for non-disclosure of important information.

In the US, due diligence became a common term and practice due to the passage of the Securities Act of 1933. Stockbrokers have the obligation to completely disclose material information that is related to the financial instruments that they are offering. Without this disclosure, stockbrokers could be liable for a criminal offense.

But the authors of the Securities Act know that the full disclosure obligation could leave stockbrokers weak against unfair prosecution if they have failed to disclose materials that they did not possess.

To protect the stockbrokers, the Act added a legal defense, which states that as long as the brokers performed due diligence in evaluating companies whose stocks they were selling, and completely disclosed their results to investors, they cannot be held liable for any information not discovered during the process.

The Process of Due Diligence

Here is a step-by-step process for conducting due diligence when you are searching for a potential addition to your dividend portfolio. Aside from dividend equities, you can also use this process for evaluating real estate, debt instruments, and other forms of investments.

Step 1 - Check the Total Value (Capitalization) of the Business

The very first step in performing due diligence for your potential dividend investments is to check how big the business is. Basically, the market capitalization of the company will allow you to assess the volatility of its stocks, the possible size of the end markets of the business, and how wide the ownership could be.

For instance, mega cap and large cap businesses tend to have more established revenue streams and a diverse investor base. This translates to less volatility.

On the other hand, small cap and mid cap businesses may only cater to specific market areas, and could have regular fluctuations in their earnings and share price.

Once you begin examining profit and revenue numbers, the market capitalization will provide you better insights.

Step 2 - Take a Look at Margin Trends, Profit, and Revenue

In conducting due diligence for dividend investment, it is ideal to begin with the profit margin and revenue trends. It is crucial for any dividend investment to understand the gross revenue, profit margins, and ROE of the company. You should also check if the company is growing or downsizing.

Be sure to check the profit margins to see if they are rising, plummeting, or have simply plateaued. Many dividend investors prefer companies with profit margins equal to 50 or higher. This piece of information is crucial for the succeeding steps.

Step 3 - Benchmark the Company with Competitors and Industries

After checking the size of the company and making a sense of how much cash it can generate, the next step is to check the industries it is operating in as well as its competitors. Remember, each business is partially defined by the competition.

Be sure to compare the profit margins of two to three competitors. Checking out the major competitors in every line of business could help you in estimating the size of the end markets for the company's products or services.

- Can you consider the business as a leader in the industry?
- What is the current status of its industry?
- Is it growing?
- Could the company's position in the industry drastically change in the next five to 10 years?

You can search for information about competitors in company profiles on many research resources, often along with a comprehensive list of specific metrics filled in for the company you are looking into and its main competitors.

If you are still not certain of the business model of the company, you must look to fill the unknown details in this step before you proceed. There are instances where investigating the competitors may help you to better understand the business of your target company.

Step 4 - Study the Valuation Multiples

The next step is to take a closer look at the details of P/S ratio, PEGs ratio, and P/E ratio, and other relevant figures. Be sure to include the figures not only for your target competitor but also for its competitors.

Be sure to note any significant discrepancies between competitors for a more comprehensive review. Many investors discover more potential dividend investments in this step. But don't easily abandon your original target.

Looking into the P/E ratios will form the initial basis for studying the valuations. Even though earnings can and will affect the volatility, valuations that are based on current estimates or trailing earnings can be used as a way to measure several or direct competition.

You can compare the basic growth stock and value stock alongside the general sense on the level of expectation built into the company. Basically, it is a good idea to assess the net earnings of the company within a specific period (commonly five years) to make sure that you are looking into the latest figures (and the one you have used to compute the P/E) is more stable, and not affected by a one-time charge for adjustment.

The P/E is not a standalone metric, but rather it is used alongside revenue ratio, the enterprise multiple, and P/B ratio. These multiples underscore the company valuation as it relates to the balance sheet, annual revenues and debt volume. Because the range in these values varies from one sector to another, it is vital to study the same figures for some competitors.

Lastly, checking the PEG ratio will allow you to look into the projection for possible earnings in the future and how it compares to the actual earnings multiple in the present.

In some sectors, this ratio could be less than one, while in other areas, this could be as much as 10 or higher. Shares with PEG ratios close to one are regarded as fairly valued under normal conditions in the market.

Step 5 - Review the Stock Ownership and Management

Is the business still managed by its founders? Or has the business hired executives to professional run the enterprise? Take note that the age of the business is a vital factor here, as younger companies have the tendency to have more of the founding members still playing vital roles.

Read the profiles of business executives to check what type of expertise and experience they have. You can find this information on SEC filings and company websites.

Also, check if the founders and business executives still hold a high percentage of stocks, and verify the volume of the float held by institutional investors. This is important to check because it shows how much analyst coverage that the business can take advantage as well as other factors that can affect the volumes of the trade in the market.

Low ownership of shares among business executives is a red flag, while high ownership of shares among top managers is a good sign. Stockholders tend to be best served if people running the company also have their own stake in the stock performance.

Step 6 - Examine the Company's Balance Sheet

An entire book could be devoted just to discuss the balance sheet. However, for the initial due diligence, a light examination can do the job. Find the summarized balance sheet of the company you are looking into and check the general level of assets and liabilities.

Be sure to pay attention to the company's capacity to pay short-term liabilities (cash levels) and the volume of long-term debt held by the business.

High volume of debt doesn't necessarily mean that the business is in bad shape. This still depends on the business model of the company. But be sure to check the agency ratings for the company bonds.

Also, check if the company is capable of generating enough cash to service its debt and issue dividend payouts. Some businesses (and sectors) require intensive capital, while others only need skeletal resources to operate.

Check the D/E ratio to see if the company has positive equity, then compare this metric with the company's competitors so you can gain a better perspective. Basically, the more cash a business can generate, the better the investment.

Try to figure out the reason behind if the figures in the top line (stockholders equity, total liabilities, and total assets) changed drastically from one year to another. Read the footnotes in the financial statements so you can understand the situation of the business.

The company might be whittling away at important capital resources, accumulating retained earnings, or preparing a new product.

Step 7 - Share Price History

In this step, you should start looking into how long all shares of classes are trading including both long-term and short-term price movement. Check if the share price has been steady, smooth, volatile, or choppy. Also check the share price in different time horizons - 3 months, 6 months, 1 year, 3 years, 5 years, and 10 years. Is it falling or rising? Does the profit trends and history match with each other?
This will show you what type of profit experience the average stockholder has seen that can affect the future movement of stocks. Bear in mind that stocks that are constantly volatile tend to have short-term stockholders that could add extra risk factors to specific investors.

Step 8 - Dilution Possibilities and Stock Options

Savvy dividend investors should next look into 10-K and 10-Q reports. Check the quarterly SEC filings of the company to see all outstanding share options and the projected conversion considering a range of stock prices in the future.

You can use this to help you understand how the share count may change under various price points. Is it possible for the company to achieve a secondary offering?

Even though employee stock options are strong motivators, be wary of any formal investigations that have been launched into shady practices such as options backdating.

Step 9 - Read Expert Projections

This step requires extra effort in the investigation. You should learn the consensus of stock analysts for profit estimates, revenue, and earnings growth for at least two years ahead.

Try to make sense of the discussions involving long-term trends that affect the sector and company-specific details about new products/services, intellectual property, joint ventures, and partnerships.

Probably, news about new business products or service first attracted you towards the stock, and now could be the time to assess it more fully with the help of all the information you have gathered so far.

Step 10 - Analyze Short and Long-Term Risks

Reserving this important piece at the end of the due diligence process will ensure that investors will always remember the risks that come with investment. Make certain that you understand both company-specific and industry-wide risks.

Is the company facing regulatory or legal concerns or just a spotty record with business managers? Is the business implementing eco-friendly policies? And what type of long-term risks could lead from it following green policies?

As an investor, you must play the devil's advocate preparing for worst-case scenarios and their possible effect on the stock. How would the company survive if a new competitor brings a better product or a new product fails?

How can you manage the downside risk? For dividend bonds, how would a decline in interest rates affect the capacity of the instrument to grow money and make money?

After completing these steps, you must be able to understand what the business is doing so far, and how it could fit into your investment strategy.

Eventually, you will have your own metrics that you can follow in performing your due diligence, but following these guidelines must save you from missing something that can be vital for your decision.

Other Important Source of Information in Researching for Stock Dividends

Annual Reports

The annual report of a company is one of the best sources of information. This will provide you with vital information about the company such as:

- Core business performance
- Business strategy
- Whether the business is making profits or losing money
- Future prospects

You may find it overwhelming to read the company annual reports, so we have specified the vital things that you must look out for.

Track Record

Make sure that the activities included in the annual report are the same as what the business said it will do in the report of the previous year. Check if the current strategy is similar as described in the past statement or report. If the strategy has changed, think how will it affect the performance of your investment.

Also, consider the ultimate goals of the company. Are the activities of the company aligned with its goals? For example, did the company say it would develop technology for the insurance industry, but is now considering accounting software for the pharmaceutical sector?

Important Strategic Acquisitions

In some instances, 'strategic acquisitions' could detract from stockholder value. When the company is expanding by acquiring other companies, you should look at the effect and check if it can add value to the company.

For instance, will the new business produce new products or services, develop new technologies or provide access to new markets? This can really affect the stock price.

Profits and Loss

In reviewing the financial side of the annual report, you should carefully assess the actual profit of the company and its source. Did the business make a profit or loss?

If the company is losing money did the management give a reason for it? Established companies should be already making profits, while startup companies usually don't make money during their early years. In this case, the management may indicate in the yearly report when they are expecting the business to make revenue.

Available Cash for Operations

Don't forget to take a look at the cash flow of the company. Is the company using its own money or has it accessed additional funding through loans or through the issuance of securities that can be converted into shares later on? If the company has approved the issuance of additional shares in the current year, have these affected the shares of current investors?

Research & Development Results

Also, check if the money invested in research and development activities has resulted in tangible outcomes such as the development of high technology product or first sale of a software application. This also involves entering into partnership or understanding with another company to use the technology it has developed.

Enough Cash Supply

You should also check the expenditures of the company. Evaluate if the company will have enough cash on hand until profits start to be generated. Without enough cash supply, how will the company meet its requirements? Can it access credit offers or will it try to raise more money from investors?

Annual reports are typically available on the website of the company for download. Most businesses are happy to send you a printed copy of their annual report upon request. But this depends on the company. You can instead directly contact the company if you are not sure.

Consider the annual report as the report card for dividend stock companies. By assessing its performance over the previous financial year, you can decide if the company is worthy to be included in your dividend portfolio.

Interesting Fact #8

Stock trading in England started when King William tried to raise money for England's wars in 1693, and English stock companies followed suit very quickly. Trading first started on the Royal Exchange, but the first stockbrokers were so rude that they were banned. Because of this, they started to trade in coffeehouses along Exchange Alley, which quickly led to the establishment of the London Stock Exchange.

Chapter 8

Dividend Reinvestment Programs (DRIP)

A dividend reinvestment program (DRIP) is a program offered by a company, which allows you to reinvest their cash dividends into added shares or fractional shares.

Many DRIPs will allow you to buy shares at zero commission and at a huge discount to the present stock price. Most companies also don't allow reinvestments lower than $10.

DRIPs are offered by dividend companies that provide shareholders the option of reinvesting the amount of a specified dividend by buying more shares. Basically, when dividends are paid, they are received by stockholders as a direct deposit into their bank account or a check sent to their home or office.

Take note that shares that are purchased through a DRIP usually come from the own reserve of the company. Hence, they are not marketable through stock exchanges. Shares should be directly redeemed via the company.

While you will not actually receive the dividends, you still need to report it as taxable income. When a company is offering a DRIP, you can set it up through a brokerage as most brokers allow dividend payments for reinvestment in the shares of any stock held in an investment profile.

Types of DRIPs

Reinvestment programs are now very popular among dividend investors. Hence, more companies are setting up their DRIPs. However, not all reinvestment plans are designed in the same way.

Direct DRIPs

Dividend companies that are running their own reinvestment programs will have a specific department (usually Investor Relations) to handle all aspects of the plan. Some companies allow individuals to buy company shares (to open a DRIP account) directly via this department without going through stock brokers.

Third-Party DRIPs

While most companies choose to operate their own reinvestment plans, other companies find the cost too high. As an alternative, they tap transfer agents or third parties who usually act on behalf of the company to manage all aspects of their DRIP.

Broker DRIPs

Another way to sign up for a reinvestment plan is through a brokerage. Due to the fact that not all companies have set up their own DRIP, some broker firms fill this void so investors can avail of DRIP perks at a fraction or even zero cost.

But you should take note that broker DRIPs usually allow only dividend reinvestment and offer no cash buying option. And of course, broker firms are also businesses that need to make revenue. So they usually only provide this special service for people who are already using their account for commissioned stock trades.

Benefits of DRIPs to the Company

Companies that are paying dividends can receive several benefits when they choose to run DRIPs.

Basically, if shares are purchased from the company for a DRIP, this will generate more capital for the company.

Meanwhile, stockholders who take part in a DRIP are less likely to sell their stocks even when the market plummets. This is due to the fact that the reinvested dividends are not as liquid as shares purchased in the stock market. Moreover, most investors easily recognize the role that their dividends play in their investment's long-term growth.

Benefits of DRIPs to the Investors

There are several benefits of buying shares through a reinvestment program. Basically, DRIPs can provide you an easy way to acquire more shares without the need to pay commission or brokerage fees.

Many companies are offering shares at a discount via their reinvestment program from 1 per cent to 10 per cent off the present price. Between price cutoff and zero commission, the cost basis for holding the shares can be remarkably lower if the shares were acquired in the open stock market.

On the other hand, the impact of automatic reinvestment is the largest advantage in the long-term. When your dividends increase, you can receive an increasing amount on every share you own. You can also use these shares so you can buy a bigger number of shares.

Eventually, this can boost the potential total return of the investment. Remember, you can buy more shares if the price of the stock decreases. On the other hand, the long-term potential for bigger gains also increase.

Downsides of DRIPs

Before you sign up for the reinvestment program offered by the dividend company, you should first understand the few disadvantages of DRIPs in general.

Primarily, those who are value investing will easily see a disadvantage with the reinvestment program, which falls on the minimal discretion on the price you are paying for new shares.

Under a DRIP, the purchase will be automatic and follows a price that is established by the current market price at dividend time. Whether or not this is a disadvantage really depends on how you perceive things. Just bear in mind that the acquired shares through the DRIP will be purchased at any stage of the market cycle. There will be times that you will buy shares at a very low price, while there will be instances that they are too expensive. The sure thing is, they will not even out.

Underwritten DRIPs

For companies who need a significant amount of capital, it is ideal for the shareholders to take part in the DRIP. While this is possible, it is not practical. So, some companies arrange to set up underwritten DRIPs.

In effect, the shareholders who choose to take part in the DRIP will receive payment in form of shares. On the other hand, the rest of the shares will be sold to another group under the terms of the underwriting policy. The cash that the company raises from the sale will be used to issue cash dividend to those shareholders who don't like additional shares.

In this case, the company has declared a dividend without paying one. Basically, this is a ridiculous practice, because shareholder interest is compromised. Be sure to stay away from companies that are underwriting their DRIPs.

The Impact of DRIP to the Stock Price

In a company-run DRIP the shares are issued from the own share reserves of the firm. If investors like to sell any shares acquired via DRIP, they can only sell them back to the company. Hence, a DRIP is operated by the business so it doesn't have any significant impact on the stock price of the shares in the market.

On the other hand, a DRIP operated by a brokerage firm purchases the shares directly through the secondary market. Since these shares are both sold and bought at the prevailing prices, a broker-operated DRIP will have the same impact on share prices as a regular buy/sell transaction in the open stock market.

Starting a DRIP Account

Getting started with a DRIP will require some effort. Basically, you should find dividend-paying companies that have DRIPs. The internet can significantly help you in looking for companies that have DRIPs.

After verifying that your company has a DRIP, you should confirm who is running the plan - the company or a third party? Then, you may need to buy company shares so you can set up your account.

To be eligible for a DRIP, you might be required by the company operating the plan to have your name registered in the stock certificate.

Take note that shares held in a brokerage account are rarely registered in the stockholder's name and are rather added in the street name. This makes it easier for the company because they don't need to phone brokerage firm to verify ownership.

The specific features of DRIPs may vary from one company to another. For instance, some companies allow optional cash purchases aside from reinvested dividends, while others only allow stockholders to buy shares based on their dividends. Be sure to clarify this fine detail before you open an account for a DRIP.

How Can Taxes Affect Your Drip Investment

Some investors wrongly think that their shares acquired through DRIPs are not taxable. This is a misconception mainly due to the fact that investors are not receiving a cash dividend per se. As a matter of fact, while DRIPs are attractive because of their cost-effective approach to investing, they are still subject to tax.

Even though reinvested, there is still an actual cash dividend that is considered an income so it is subject for taxation. And like any stock, capital gains from shares acquired via DRIP are not calculated and taxed until the shares are finally sold, normally after a few years.

Managing Volatility through DRIPs and Dollar Cost Averaging

You don't need a lot of capital to begin dividend investing thanks to DRIPs. You can start with next to nothing and end up with significant holdings plus passive income. A reinvestment program makes it possible to invest as low as $30 or $50 and acquire shares directly from the company without the need to open a brokerage account and pay broker's commissions or fees.

Not so many people are aware of direct reinvestment plans because no one is advertising them. Companies are also prohibited from advertising their reinvestment programs under SEC rules.

There is no such thing as zero-risk investment. Any form of investment has a certain level of risk. However, most investors usually get burned trying to sense the direction of the market. You can manage this risk through a reinvestment program. After a certain amount of time, your conservative investment strategy already has built your wealth by consistently investing the money that you might have spent on something you didn't actually need.

Hence, DRIPs can provide you access to the same level of risk-reducing strategies that are usually reserved for the big players. You can buy shares on the market dips and get holdings from a lot of diverse companies.

Moreover, you are less likely to react emotionally to financial updates and there is no need to worry too much about your broker. The reinvestment program will keep on adding shares that you own until you increase your wealth.

Signing up for a reinvestment program will allow you to take advantage of dollar cost averaging. This will let you invest as low as $25 in every company whenever you have some spare money to do so.

Through dollar cost averaging, you can ditch the guesswork. Even when the market is down, your reinvestment strategy will allow you to buy more shares that it would when the market is following an upward trend.

Dollar cost averaging is an efficient and effective long-term investment strategy. It makes saving easy especially if you are gunning for retirement holdings and income. All you need is a small yet consistent flow of money. This will help you stand your ground despite market changes. This is how savvy dividend investors place a cap on their upside and basically lose money in the stock market.

Using this approach, the cost will be considerably less compared to the trading price of the shares during the time you are investing. This is because you are automatically buying fewer shares when the stocks are selling at higher prices and sell more when the prices are lower. Definitely, this strategy is only ideal for those who are investing with a long-term outlook, usually not shorter than five years. This will not produce results for traders who are looking for quick cash.

With a reinvestment plan, you can put the dollar-cost averaging on autopilot. You can just invest a specific dollar amount regularly. The usual outcome is that you can obtain more shares at lower prices then fewer shares at higher prices. You can do this regularly with a no-fee DRIP and you can build wealth in the most cost-efficient approach.

Not similar to the conventional way of investing that is based on acquiring a specific number of shares, DRIP investment is based on dollar amounts. A zero-fee reinvestment program makes it easy to invest even small amounts regularly. Dollar cost averaging will also impose discipline on your investment because you decide how many dollars you want to invest on a schedule that you have determined ahead.

How Dollar Cost Averaging Can Boost Your Dividend Income

The example below will help you understand how your dividend income can be significantly improved if you sign up with a reinvestment program and use dollar cost averaging. In this example, we assume that you are investing in a stock that has zero fees. Let's say you are investing $100 every quarter and acquire however many shares your investment will buy at the present share price. Take a look at what will happen over time.

Dollar-Cost Average

Invest	$/Share	Share	Invest	$/Share	Share
$100	$12	8.3333	$100	$35	2.8571
$100	$9	11.1111	$100	$30	3.3333
$100	$30	3.3333	$100	$12	8.3333
$100	$35	2.8571	$100	$9	11.1111
$400		25.6348	$400		25.6348

Invest	$/Share	Share	Invest	$/Share	Share
$100	$9	11.1111	$100	$30	3.3333
$100	$12	8.3333	$100	$35	2.8571
$100	$30	3.3333	$100	$9	11.1111
$100	$35	2.8571	$100	$12	8.3333
$400		25.6348	$400		25.6348

Average price (based on the four investment prices) = $21.50
Average cost (based on the amount spent and the number of shares aquired) = $15.60

The price of the stock fluctuated between $9 and $35 with an average price of $21.50. However, the average cost per share was only $15.60 (i.e. $400/25.6348). You can buy more shares if the price is low and fewer shares if the price is high. This is precisely how you can buy low and sell high - the classic mantra in stock dividend investing.

Interesting Fact #9

Though they have the name, 'penny stocks' usually don't cost a penny. Instead, the Securities and Exchange Commission usually considers any stock under $5.00 a 'penny stock', according to sec.gov. They categorize most stocks under $5.00 with certain rules. I say 'most stocks' because when CITI was trading under $5.00, they didn't identify CITI as a penny stock, for whatever their reason. There are penny stocks that trade for a penny, but they don't have to trade for a penny to be called a 'penny stock'.

Chapter 9

How to Diversify Your Portfolio

Diversification is a risk management technique, which includes different types of investments in a portfolio. The core concept behind this strategy claims that an investment portfolio composed of diverse forms of investments shall on average, pose a lower risk and yield higher returns than any individual investment found inside the portfolio.

Diversifying your portfolio can ease out the unsystematic risk events so the instruments that are performing well can neutralize the negative performance of others. Hence, the advantages of diversification hold only if the investments in the portfolio *are not correlated with each other.*

What is Unsystematic Risk?

Unsystematic risk, also known as residual risk or specific risk, is often described as the risk that is inherent in a business or industry investment. The types of unsystematic risk involve a new competitor in the market with the potential to take considerable market share from the business.

Even though investors may be able to project some sources of this inherent risk, it is not always certain to be aware of how or when the risk could affect your investment.

For instance, an investor in aged care stocks might be aware that a huge shift in retirement policy is inevitable. However, there is no way to know in advance the details of the new policy and how aged care companies and consumers will react.

Mathematical models and market studies have shown that keeping a well-diversified portfolio of 25 to 30 stocks could yield the most cost-effective level of reducing risk. Investing in more securities could yield further diversification benefits but in a remarkably smaller rate.

You can also maximize the benefits of diversification if you invest in foreign securities because they have the tendency to be less affected with your investments in the domestic market.

For instance, a financial crisis in the US economy may not reach the Australian economy. Hence, having Australian investments can provide you with an added layer of protection against the possible losses due to the US downturn.

Many individual investors have limited capital and so you may find it not easy to build a well-balanced and diversified portfolio. This is the reason why mutual funds are growing in popularity. Acquiring shares in a mutual fund can provide you with a more affordable way to diversify your portfolio.

Why Should You Build a Diversified Dividend Portfolio?

If you invest all of your money in one business, despite the promise of low risk and high returns, you will likely yield returns that are considerably different compared to the performance of the market in general.

Many investors don't have the stomach for such volatility, especially because there are several unforeseen events that may happen to put your investment at risk of being lost permanently.

Do you still remember Lehman Brothers? What about Enron? Placing all your eggs in one basket can have disastrous effects.

On the other hand, let's say you have the means to buy shares of each stock in the market. For each company or industry in your portfolio that is struggling, there is a possibility that there are more industries in your portfolio that are growing.

Hence, you don't need to depend on any single company to boost your investment returns and dividend income. Your portfolio can sustain a few unfortunate events because you have a diverse form of investments across several businesses.

As long as the United States continues to exist and thrive, there will be virtually no reason for your portfolio to completely lose its value. The stock market has been appreciating over the years and there are no indications that this will be disrupted anytime soon.

A diversified and well-balanced portfolio can help you diversify your risk exposure and achieve your investment goals. Building a portfolio begins with an understanding of the primary risk factors that affect the volatility and profitability of your dividend investments.

Important Risk Factors to Consider in Building Your Portfolio

Below are the most important factors that can influence the returns of your portfolio relative to the returns in the market:
- The number of holdings
- The amount of financial leverage each holding has
- The correlation between holdings
- The size of the market capitalization of each holding

These risk factor can remarkably affect the performance of a portfolio, especially during bearish markets. Many investors are usually not aware that they are betting against their portfolios until it benefits them.

As an example, let's say that around 50% of your portfolio is invested in small-cap energy stocks with high financial leverage. As oil production and prices followed an upward trend, your portfolio has received excellent returns with lower volatility as of late 2014.

Many investors would often cite their skills instead of luck when the results are favorable. But this portfolio was nothing more than a factor bet on the sector and good conditions in the market.

When the price of oil plummets and there are fewer credits available to small-cap companies, the portfolio would lose a lot of its value.

The main point of building a portfolio is to diversify the factor bets that we cannot forecast or control and concentrate our returns on the performance of individual businesses.

The Number of Holdings

Many successful investment firms are running portfolios that are considered as concentrated. For instance, the lucrative Berkshire Hathaway has several holdings that go beyond the 10 per cent of the overall value of its stock portfolio. The firm led by Warren Buffet invests with conviction behind the best stocks in the market.

Chances are, you don't have the resources, insights, and connections of a big investment firm to successfully run a concentrated investment portfolio.

As such, it is ideal for individual investors to spread their bets over a reasonable range of various stocks so you can avoid shooting yourself in the foot with stock investments that go wayward.

The fewer holdings you have, the bigger chance that your portfolio can deviate from the returns in the market. Hence, it is crucial to determine the right number of holdings you should have to maximize the benefits of diversification.

It is interesting to note that professional stock market researchers tried to answer this question over half of the century. For instance, the American Association of Individual Investors (AAII) published an article which contends:

> "Holding a single stock rather than a perfectly diversified portfolio increases annual volatility by roughly 30%...Thus, the single-stock investor will experience annual returns that average a whopping 35% above or below the market - with some years closer to the market and some years further from the market."

This institutional research went on to cite that as a general rule, company-specific (diversified) risk could be reduced by the following figures:
- 95% risk reduced when you hold 400 stocks
- 90% risk reduced when you hold 100 stocks
- 80% risk reduced when you hold 25 stocks

Another study was published in 2014 entitled "Equity Portfolio Diversification: How Many Stocks are Enough? Evidence from Five Developed Markets."

This research discovered that a higher number of stocks are required to diversify the risk during the financial downturn. In this kind of economic climate, the correlation between stocks is usually the highest.

In the US, the study concluded that to be certain of decreasing 90% of the risk, 90% of the time, the number of stocks required on average is around 55. This can however increase to around 110 stocks during times of economic turmoil.

With the findings from these studies, the sweet spot would seem in between 25 and 100 stocks. But if you throw in math into the mix, you should also consider factors that are unique to your financial constraints - trading cost, availability of resources and time for due diligence, and the size of your portfolio.

The effect of trading costs on your total returns will be bigger if your portfolio is smaller. If you have a small account, you may need to buy dividend ETFs instead of individual stocks so you can easily achieve diversification and save money on trading costs. You need less time in performing due diligence if you own more positions.

Although this is subjective, holding between 20 and 65 stocks can provide you a reasonable balance considering the factors of available time for due diligence, saving money from trading costs and the need to diversify.

Concentrating on higher quality stocks with a narrower range of possible outcomes can help in reducing risk to support a more focused portfolio. Meanwhile, a portfolio that is filled with risky stocks may choose a direction towards diversification with around 65 holdings.

Many individual investors prefer to roughly equate their positions because it can be difficult to know which holdings will perform well in the long run. Eventually, you have a unique opinion as an individual investor on how much diversification is sufficient and how much risk you can tolerate.

Diversification in the Industry Level

While adding more stocks in your portfolio can help you diversify the risk, there are still investors who end up with portfolios that are not well diversified because they follow strict investing rules (buying only stocks with P/E ratio less than 12x) or specific types of stocks (consumer products with household brands).

But holding on several stocks with the same characteristics will not help you maximize the benefits of diversification. This is due to the fact that stocks from similar industries are usually sensitive to the same factors and they usually have the same inherent risks.

Your investment portfolio could drastically underperform in the market when a shared factor like oil price or interest rates becomes unfavorable. Choosing stocks from various industries and sectors can help in diversifying the risk because if some industries are struggling, others might be doing well.

Many savvy dividend investors prefer to invest no more than 25% of their portfolio into a single sector, and try to own company stocks with minimum overlap into their actual operations.

There's no surefire way to determine which areas of the market would come in or out of favor, so sector diversification is crucial. But sector diversification must not come at the expense of contradicting principles of valuation or reaching beyond your comfort zone.

Consumer staples account for around 7% of the S&P500, but it doesn't mean you should buy stocks from this sector if you can't find one that is priced attractively. Moreover, you must not diversify into an industry or sector that is outside your circle of competence.

For instance, many conservative dividend investors have few investments in the technology sector because it evolves at a fast pace. It can be challenging to predict which companies will still be relevant for the next several years.

The takeaway here is that you must be deliberate with your diversification across business models and sectors. You still need to think through your investments. Choose market sectors that you are comfortable with and carefully evaluate each possible dividend investment as you gear towards diversification.

Financial Leverage

Using financial leverage for your investment portfolio can help you magnify your returns. This is one of the important factors that you need to understand when you are looking for safe stocks. The higher the debt volume of the company, the higher the stock price may fluctuate depending on the economic and business climate.

Hence, companies with huge debt loads and are naturally cyclical often have more volatile stocks. Some of the highly leveraged, lower quality may struggle if interest rates suddenly rise and credit conditions become stricter.

In building a portfolio, it is crucial to be aware of the general credit quality of your holdings. For many forms of investments, it is ideal to see an investment grade credit rating, strong coverage ratios, and no more than 50 per cent free cash flow generation.

Size of Investment

Historically, businesses with small market caps have shown better share price volatility compared to businesses with large market caps. Large companies are more liquid because of the availability of buyers and sellers.

If you enter into an order to sell or buy stocks of Apple, there should be someone on the other side of the counter who will agree to your asking price for the trade to proceed.

Companies with smaller market caps ($2 billion and under) could have much less liquidity in comparison to big cap companies. With fewer trades in the market, it is often difficult to move in and out of positions. Also, the spread between the buyer and the seller could become quite wide.

With less active trading liquidity, companies with small caps can easily outperform or underperform big cap stocks in various market settings. Small cap stocks also have high volatility because their businesses are usually less diversified compared to big caps.

Time Horizon and Price Volatility

Aside from the four risk factors discussed above, you should also understand price volatility or beta. This will help you take advantage of their long-term holding periods so you can enhance your dividend portfolios.

Beta will help you measure the volatility of the stock price to the market. By default, the market has a 1.0 beta, and individual stocks are ranked based on how much they deviate from the market in general.

Stocks with beta of more than 1.0 swings more than the market over time. When a stock has moved below the market, the beta of the stock is lower than 1.0.

The risk factors discussed above largely affects the beta of the stock. Smaller companies with less predictable business models and high volume of financial leverage will normally have higher betas.

It is crucial for investors to understand the different emotional tendencies and risk tolerances despite the fact that beta is backward-looking.

An investment portfolio filled with stocks that have beta values higher than 1.0 will likely move a lot compared to a portfolio that is filled with stocks with low beta.

You should also take note that beta is based on near-term price volatility that is not usually affected by business fundamentals. To put it simply, for long-term investors, a low or high beta does not indicate if an investment will be profitable over the next five years.

One advantage of individual investors is the capacity to hold stocks for a longer duration to allow strong underlying fundamentals to be reflected in the price of the stock. Building your dividend investment portfolio follows a slower pace.

Basically, it is ideal to own shares of high-quality growth stocks at a reasonable price than to stay on the sidelines trying to beat the quarterly profits game or time the market. The time horizon should be on your side and not against you.

Diversifying Your Investment through Dividend ETFs

Many dividend investors diversify their portfolios through dividend exchange traded funds (ETFs). Basically, ETFs allow you to invest in a basket of high-dividend paying stocks.

Dividend ETFs are mainly established to achieve high yields when investing in high-dividend-paying real-estate investment trusts (REITs), preferred stocks, or common stocks.

Most dividend ETFs may contain only US stocks or they could be composed of international ETFs with a global focus. Many indexes used to build the dividend ETFs contain stocks with higher than average liquidity and above-market dividend yields. But take note that these will vary based on the fund manager of the ETF and their particular style.

Dividend ETFs are managed passively, which means they are monitoring a particular index, that is often filtered based on quantitative criteria to involve companies with a solid track record of dividend increases and more established blue-chip companies that are basically regarded to carry minimal risk.

The expense to dividend ratio must be lower or at least at par to the most affordable no-load mutual funds. By definition, you can buy or redeem no-load mutual funds after a specific duration of time without sales or commission charge. In general, dividend ETFs are ideal for risk-averse stock investors who are mainly seeking income.

Dividend ETFs Vs Other ETFs

In general, ETFs will provide you the opportunity to diversify an index fund and enable minimal trades as they don't have minimum deposit requirements. Moreover, the expense ratios of ETFs are lower compared to average mutual funds for commonly available ETFs in the stock market.

Adding dividend ETFs to your overall investment portfolio will provide you robust yet safe financial strategy, but there are also other forms of ETFs that you may consider and include in your portfolio for further diversification.

For instance, an Initial Public Offering (IPO) ETF can be enticing for investors who like to try investing in startup companies who are opening their business to the public. You can diversify your investment across different IPOs from different industries and sectors.

The benefits of investing in IPO ETFs are grounded in the upsides from possible beneficial growth in the stock price. However, initial IPO success doesn't guarantee stability and growth because the value of the holdings may decrease eventually. And of course, very few startup companies will offer dividend payouts on the onset so you have to think carefully of including this in your portfolio.

Meanwhile, Index ETFs monitor a benchmark index such as the S&P 500. You can trade index ETFs all day long on a primary stock exchange and you can take advantage of exposure to different securities in a single transaction.

Depending on the ETF you are tracking, index ETFs may include both American and international markets, different asset classes or specific sectors.

Lastly, the ETF of ETFs is mainly tracking other ETFs instead of an index or an underlying stock. This special type of ETF will provide you more opportunities for diversification compared to other ETFs.

ETF of ETFs are managed actively similar to funds in comparison with other ETFs that are managed passively. Thus, they can be designed to consider other factors such as your time horizon and risk tolerance. This approach will provide you with wide exposure to strategies across various class assets, immediate diversification, and minimal charges.

Building a dividend portfolio is part science, part art. This significantly depends on your available capital, risk tolerance, and goals. Taking a closer look at the important risk factors could affect the returns of a portfolio and could help you avoid taking unnecessary risk.

Below are risk management pointers that you should bear in mind:
- Stocks must be diversified across various sectors and industries, with no specific sector composing more than 25% of the value of the portfolio.
- Stocks with high financial leverage and higher volatility usually pose a greater risk for stockholders.
- Depending on due diligence constraints and portfolio size, holding between 20 and 60 well-balanced stocks is reasonable for individual investors.
- Small cap stocks have high volatility compared to large cap stocks
- A stock beta will help you determine the volatility of the stock in relation to the market
- You are basically speculating if you invest with a time horizon in months or quarters

As an individual investor, you should review your personal goals and keep the above factors in mind.

Interesting Fact #10

While it may be true that some people get lucky and actually make money in penny stocks, these stories are rare. Remember that there are a lot of scam artists out there - if you have ever heard of the phrase "pump and dump" that's where the term comes from. Experienced people in the business of scamming others with penny stocks can easily 'hype up' a random ticker symbol and when everyone is in, they will go ahead and sell, and leave you penniless.

Chapter 10

When to Sell a Dividend Stock

Most literature about dividend investing focuses on what stocks to buy and how to build your dividend portfolio. The area of selling stocks is not usually discussed, because many investors are more excited about buying stocks than selling.

Our minds are more focused on how much profit we can make in stock investing, and how our dividend payments will grow. If you sell a stock, it is either you need to use the money in your investment or you think that there is better investment available elsewhere. This is arguably boring compared to the prospect of making profits purchasing new shares.

Two Major Reasons to Sell Dividend Stocks

There are two major reasons to help you decide if it is time to sell your stocks:
- If the stocks are selling above fair value
- If the stocks are on the verge of losing or have already lost their competitive advantage

Why Sell Overpriced Stocks?

It is ideal to sell dividend stocks with a normalized P/E ratio above 40. Historically, stocks with high P/E ratio have significantly underperformed shares with low P/E ratios. The Compustat-Faceset image below shows the performance of stocks with high P/E ratios compared to stocks with low P/E ratios in a period of 35 years.

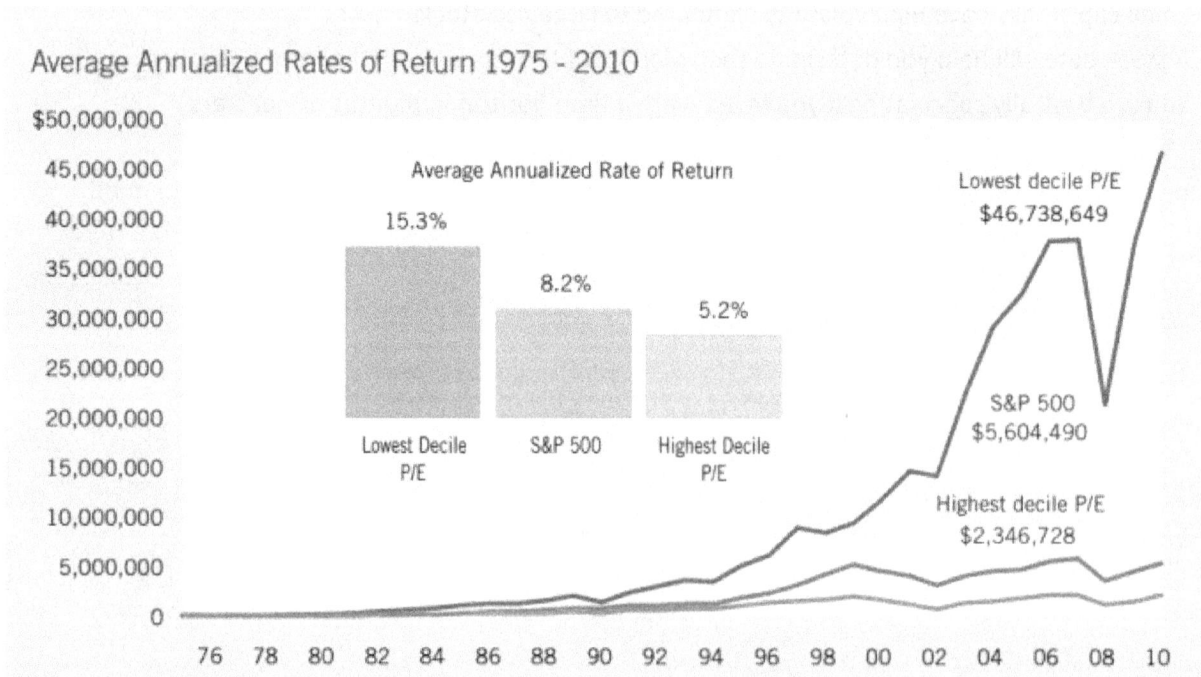

Average Annualized Rates of Return 1975 - 2010

Stocks with high price tags have considerably underperformed the stock market. The normalized P/E ratio of 40 is utilized as a cut-off because this is the nearest valuation that the whole S&P 500 has achieved. A dividend stock with P/E ratio of 40 is highly likely to be overvalued.

It is ideal to use normalized profits instead of GAAP profits. You should avoid selling stocks with P/E ratio of 40 because profits are depressed 50% because of a one-time event.

In addition, it is not ideal to sell high-cycle stocks because it has a high P/E ratio because of depressed earnings from the cyclical wave. Selling your overpriced stocks will move your investments to a fair value dividend stocks that will reward you with both dividend and price growth.

Why Sell Stocks that Have Lost their Competitive Advantage?

Dividend stocks that have either eliminated or cut their dividend payouts have either permanently or temporarily affected investor dividend income. The main objective of holding onto high-quality dividend growth stocks is to ensure that the dividend stock will steadily grow over time. It doesn't make sense to hold onto stocks that cut or eliminate dividend payments.

Companies that reduce or cut dividend payouts send a warning signal to investors. This shows that the companies are not capable of maintaining its present cash flow.

This basically means the company's competitive advantage has reduced or absolutely disrupted and lost. In any case, you should move your investment into high-quality stocks that will regularly increase dividend payouts.

The strategy of holding unto stocks that have reduced or cut their dividend payouts is backed by historical data. In a 40-year period, stocks that reduce or cut their dividends generate an average returns of 0%.

Stocks that eliminate or reduce their dividend will provide reduced or zero returns. It is better to hold cash in an interest-growing bank account instead of owning stocks that have reduced or cut their dividend payouts. The Oppenheimer image below shows how dividend growth stocks have significantly outperformed stocks that reduce or cut their dividend payouts.

S&P 500 Index: Dividend Growers Have Outperformed with Less Risk
Risk and Return (1972–2013)

Dividend Growers and Initiators
(16.1, 10.1%)

All Dividend-Paying Stocks
(16.9, 9.3%)

Dividend Payers with no Change
(18.2, 7.7%)

Non-Dividend-Paying Stocks
(25.3, 2.3%)

Dividend Cutters or Eliminators
(25.3, 0.0%)

AVERAGE ANNUALIZED RETURN (%)

ANNUALIZED STANDARD DEVIATION

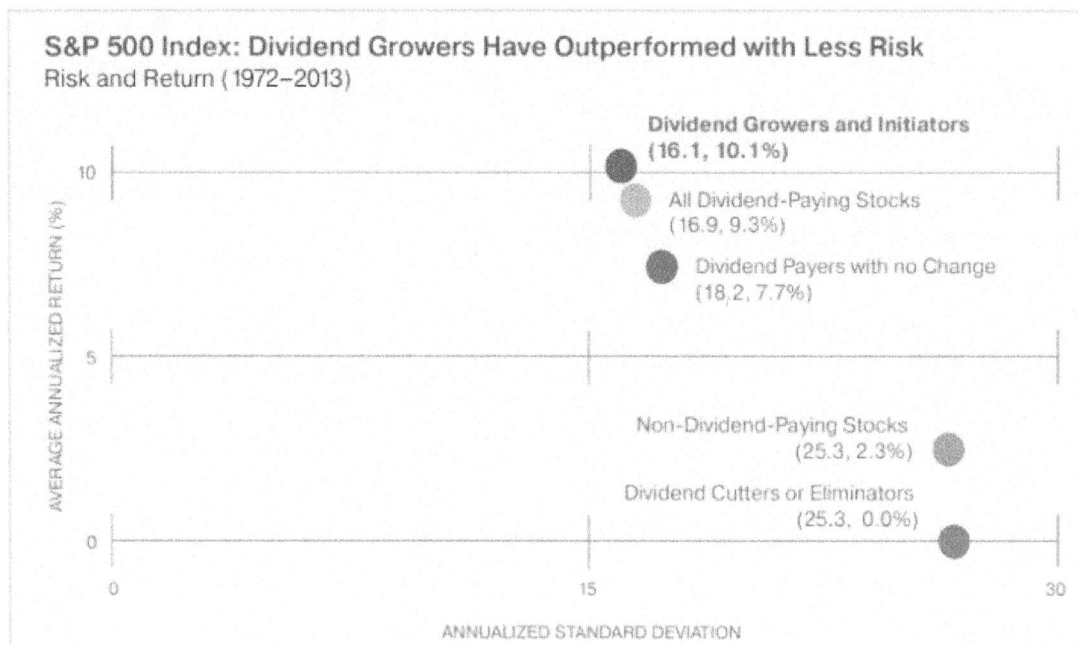

Selling Stocks Prior to Ex-Dividend Date

Bear in mind that if you sell prior to the ex-date (ex-dividend date), you are not eligible for receiving a dividend from the stocks you own.

Remember, the ex-date is the date that the company has assigned as the first day of trading in which the stocks trade without having the right for a dividend. You are still eligible for dividend payout if you sell your shares on or after this specific date.

Basically, you need to be listed on the company's date of record. This list is used to identify the company's holders of record and to authorize individuals to those whom financial reports, proxy statements, and other relevant details are sent.

If you buy shares, your name will not be instantly added to the company records. This will take around three days from the transaction date.

Hence, if the date of record is June 15, you should purchase the shares on June 12 to qualify for dividend payouts. This will make June 13 as the ex-date because this is the date directly following the last date on which you can receive dividend.

The ex-date is specified by the stock exchange or the National Association of Securities Dealers when the date of record is already set.

How Ex-Date Affect the Share Prices

Take note that a company stock will trade for less than the dividend value at the ex-date than they did the day prior. In general, if a dividend-payout distributes a huge dividend, the market could account for this dividend in the days before the ex-dividend date because of buyers still acquiring shares. There are investors who are willing to pay a high premium to be eligible for the payout.

For instance, if the stocks in a company are trading at $60 and the company announces a dividend of $6, individual investors who hold the shares past the ex-dividend date shall receive the $6, while those who sell prior to the ex-dividend date are no longer eligible for the payout.

But the company stocks might fall by around the value of the dividend, in our example, $54. There might also be an opportunity for an arbitrage in the stock market. If stocks don't fall as a result of dividend payouts, many would flock to acquire the shares for $60, receive $6, and then sell the stocks after the ex-date. So they are getting free money from the shares.

In an ideal world, investors would never have to sell their dividend stocks. Your dividend investments would continue to earn passive income as long as you hold it.

But alas, there is no surefire way to predict the future. Chances are, you will encounter and invest stocks that could eliminate or reduce their dividend payouts or become considerably overvalued.

In any case, it is ideal to reinvest the profits into stocks that are high quality but undervalued and fairly valued. Buying undervalued dividend stocks and selling overvalued dividend stocks could likely boost the dividend yield of your investment portfolio.

Even stocks with 100% payout ratio will only have 2.5 per cent yield if the P/E ratio is 40. Meanwhile, an undervalued stock will likely have better dividend yield. All things being equal, the dividend yield will be higher if the stock price of the dividend is lower.

Disposing of dividend stocks that have eliminated or canceled dividend payouts will likely increase the dividend growth rate of your dividend portfolio in the future. Savvy investors would never trust companies who decide to cut or eliminate their payouts.

You can increase the possible dividend growth rate of your general investment portfolio if you sell dividend stocks that are no longer issuing payments.

When the right time comes, investors who have a pre-established plan for selling shares can easily execute their plan. Investors who don't have a plan may prematurely sell or hold on to their shares a bit longer with the false hope that companies who eliminated their payouts will soon turn around.

A selling plan will help you prevent panic selling and will provide you with clear and solid rules on when to sell.

Interesting Fact #11

Declaring dividends without sufficient profits is illegal

Company directors issuing dividends when the company has insufficient profits don't actually have the authority to do so – if they do the dividend is illegal.

These are what's known as "ultra vires" dividends, which means 'beyond the powers'. You should ensure there are profits, and involve your accountant if required, before declaring dividends to avoid the risk of breaking the law.

Chapter 11

In this final chapter, we will take a look at the investment case study involving a middle-aged investor who has been buying dividend stocks since 2001. Let's call him Mike who is looking into the ABC Company Stocks with the following figures in 2006:

Valuation
> Dividend Yield: more than 3%
> P/E Ratio: low 20
> Forward P/E Ratio: low 20

Fundamentals
> RoE: high 15%
> EPS Growth (past 5 years): +
> EPS Growth (next 5 years): +
> Sales Growth (past 5 years): +
> Dividend Payout Ration (DPR): 33%

With Mike's experience as a dividend investor, he used different financial ratios and metrics to evaluate possible stocks for his portfolio.

Among the many available financial ratios, Mike mainly used the dividend payout ratio (DPR) to analyze the dividend stock of ABC Company. He used this metric to analyze the dollar amount of the dividend that a company is paying in accordance to its net income.

The DPR helped Mike understand the percentage of earnings that ABC company is paying to its stockholders and investors. Any money that is not paid out to shareholders or investors will be reinvested into the company operations or expansion.

While the DPR helped Mike to gain some insight about ABC company, it cannot however provide information on shareholder value. Based on his past experience, Mike doesn't use DPR as a metric to assess the viability of the company.

Mike is only using DPR if he is considering whether to invest in a profitable business that is paying dividends in comparison with a company with high potential for growth. He also used DPR as a way to compare a steady revenue or reinvestment for potential earnings in the future.

Mike's DPR Computation

Through the DPR, Mike can see how much money the business is putting back into its growth, for paying its debt, and its cash reserves. With this metric, he can compare the value of ABC company against the amount of money that is distributed to the investors and stockholders as dividends. To get the DPR, Mike reviewed the company's income statement.

To double check, Mike used a formula for computing the DPR by dividing the annual dividend paid by the net income (Dividends/Net Income = DPR).

Through this formula, Mike confirmed that ABC Company paid $1 dollar for every share in yearly dividend payouts, while the EPS was $3. Then, the DPR would be 33% or 0.33 or 1/3.

Mike's DPR Interpretation

But through experience, Mike knows that DPR interpretation is relative. In this case, ABC company has a DPR of 33%. This doesn't mean it is already a good payout or a bad one. The answer to this may vary depending on Mike's risk tolerance, personal goals, and investment strategy.

More often than not, growing companies have the tendency to retain the majority of its revenue to finance growth. Eventually, this will provide the investor with dividend in the future. However, this will come at a cost of the investor not receiving any dividend at present.

After reviewing the company profile, Mike learned that ABC Company can be considered a mature company so it has the capacity to provide higher dividends. The company has already reached the peak of its growth so it can sustain a 33% payout rate.

Mike also checked the dividend payout trend of the company over time. This helped him to know if the company has the ability to sustain its profits and thus sustain the dividend payouts.

Sustainable Growth Model for ABC Company

In looking into the financials of ABC Company, Mike also came across XYZ Company which has similar net income and ROE to the former. The only difference is in their retention ratios.

ABC Company has an ROE of 15% and returns 33% of its net income to stockholders in a dividend. Hence, the company is retaining 67% of its net income.

XYZ Company also has ROE of 15% but only returns 10% of its net income to stockholders for a retention ratio of 90%.

Mike used the sustainable growth model to do a comparative analysis of the two companies. He has learned to use this model to make estimates about the future of dividend stocks and to determine if specific stocks are risky because their dividend payouts are not sustainable.

Mike is aware that a stock that is slowly growing compared to its sustainable rate might be undervalued, or the stock market might be discounting red flags from the company. In any case, a growth rate that is below or above the sustainable rate should require more due diligence.

The result of the comparative analysis seems to make XYZ company look more attractive than ABC Company. However, this is reckless to say because it doesn't consider the benefits of a higher dividend rate that could be attractive to savvy investors.

You can modify the computation to make an estimate of the dividend growth rate of the stock that could be more important for Mike who is an income investor.

To get an estimate, Mike multiplied ROE by the payout ratio, which resulted in the sustainable growth rate that favors ABC Company.

Mike's Timing Strategy

ABC Company stocks caught Mike's attention because of the announcement of ex-dividend date where investors can receive a dividend from the company. Mike is aware that he can sell the shares a bit later after receiving the dividend.

To put it simply, Mike can choose to buy the dividend. However, Mike is also aware that this strategy is risky, since he believes the current market is relatively efficient.

In his prior trades, he learned that share prices could be pushed higher before the ex-date as investors are getting excited. On or around the payment date, the price usually plummets. So Mike made sure that before buying ABC Company stocks, he would hold on to it because of passive income and not because of the immediate dividend that he could receive.

Mike's Dividend Holding Size

Within five years of building his dividend portfolio, Mike has around 80 stocks diversified in different industries and sectors. While he has several stocks, he still investigates any stock he wants to buy like he did his first investment.

He aims to have at least 300 stocks in a 10-year time horizon, so buying ABC Company stocks is just one of the many stocks he will end up holding. So far, Mike only bought 1,000 shares of ABC Company stocks.

After buying the shares, Mike plans to monitor the performance of the stock, stay updated on news about the company, and check the daily fluctuations of the stocks. He also made sure that the commissions and trading costs are below 2% of his total purchase amount.

Mike's Dollar Cost Averaging Strategy

Mike follows dollar cost averaging for his dividend investment strategy. He is now trained in placing a specific dollar value into his dividend investments on a regular recurring schedule, which he plans to employ for his investment in ABC Company.

Mike found it helpful to follow dollar cost averaging because it allows him to be consistent and remove the emotion from investing. Because of the fixed dollar value he is investing, he can buy more ABC Company stocks if the market is lower and fewer shares if the market is higher.

Mike's Decision to Sell ABC Company Shares

After 12 years of holding ABC Company shares, Mike decided to sell all his stocks after confirming the news that the company board of directors decided to cut their dividend payouts.

As a dividend investor, Mike's primary objective is to hold onto high-quality dividend growth stocks that would steadily grow over time. Hence, ABC Company reducing their dividend payout is quite concerning.

After years of investing in dividends, Mike is already aware that companies that are cutting or even reducing their dividend payments are in some kind of distress, because they are no longer capable of sustaining their current cash flow.

Upon further investigation, Mike also learned that ABC Company already lost its competitive advantage due to a new player in the industry that is aggressively fighting for market share and making the competition more cut throat.

What's more? ABC Company's profit margins have been on the decline for 3 straight years prior to the reduction in dividend payout! This further solidified his decision to move his investment into other dividend stocks that have a high potential for dividend payouts.

Finally, you've made it!

This is the end of learning all about dividend investing, right?

Nope. Reading this book is only the start of your investment journey. Following through on the strategies and tactics that you have learned is the other part of the whole deal.

How do you feel now? Can you say that you are already confident that you can start investing in dividend stocks? I hope so because if you have truly understood the content of this book, you can easily answer yes to that.

In a while, you will feel mixed emotions once you start investing in dividend stocks. The best part is, you are now more confident because you have a guide that you can use as an easy reference whenever you have questions.

My goal is to help you decide if dividend investing is really for you, and I hope this book has provided you the knowledge you need to make that decision.

Here's to your success!

Affiliate Marketing: Learn How to Make $10,000+ Each Month On Autopilot

Are you looking for an online business that you can start today? Do you feel like no matter how hard you try - you never seem to make money online? If so, this book has you covered. If you correctly implement the strategies in this book, you can make commissions of up to $10,000 (or more) per month in extra income.

- WITHOUT creating your own products
- WITHOUT any business or management experience
- WITHOUT too much start up capital or investors
- WITHOUT dealing with customers, returns, or fulfillment
- WITHOUT building websites
- WITHOUT selling anything over the phone or in person
- WITHOUT any computer skills at all
- WITHOUT leaving the comfort of your own home

In addition, because I enrolled this book in the kindle matchbook program, **Amazon will make the kindle edition available to you for FREE** after you purchase the paperback edition from Amazon.com, saving you roughly $6.99!!

Available In Kindle, Paperback and Audio

Passive Income Ideas: 50 Ways To Make Money Online Analyzed

How many times have you started a business only to later realise it wasn't what you expected? Would you like to go into business knowing beforehand the potential of the business and what you need to do to scale it? If so, this book can help you

In Passive Income Ideas, you'll discover

- A concise, step-by-step analysis of 50 business models you can leverage to earn passive income (Including one that allows you to earn money watching TV!)
- Strategies that'll help you greatly simplify some of the business models (and in the process make them more passive!)
- What you can do to scale your earnings (regardless of which business you choose)
- Strategies you can implement to minimize the level of competition you face in each marketplace
- Myths that tend to hold people back from succeeding in their business (we debunk more than 100 such myths!)
- Well over 150 Insightful tips that'll give you an edge and help you succeed in whichever business you chose to pursue
- More than 100 frequently asked questions (with answers)

- 50 positive vitamins for the mind (in the form of inspirational quotes that'll keep you going during the tough times)
- A business scorecard that neatly summarizes, in alphabetical order, each business models score across 4 criteria i.e. simplicity, passivity, scalability and competitiveness
- …and much much more!

What's more? Because the book is enrolled in kindle matchbook program, **Amazon will make the kindle edition available to you for FREE** after you purchase the paperback edition from Amazon.com, saving you roughly $6.99!!

Available In Kindle, Paperback and Audio

Work From Home: 50 Ways To Make Money Online Analyzed

This is a **2-in-1 book bundle** consisting of the below books. Amazon will make the kindle edition available to you for FREE when you purchase the print version of this bundle from Amazon.com - **saving you roughly 35%** from the price of the individual books.

- Passive Income Ideas – 50 Ways to Make Money Online Analyzed (Part I)
- Affiliate Marketing – Learn How to Make $10,000+ Each Month on Autopilot (Part 2)

Get this bundle at a 35% discount from Amazon.com

Available In Kindle, Paperback and Audio

Dropshipping: Discover How to Make Money Online, Build Sustainable Streams of Passive Income and Gain Financial Freedom Using The Dropshipping E-Commerce Business Model

How many times have you started a business only to later realise you had to spend a fortune to get the products manufactured, hold inventory and eventually ship the products to customers all over the globe?

Would you like to start your very own e-commerce business that gets right to making money without having to deal with all of these issues? If so, this book can help you

In this book, you'll discover:

- A simple, step-by-step explanation of what the dropshipping business is all about (Chapter 1)
- 8 reasons why you should build a dropshipping business (Chapter 2)
- Disadvantages of the dropshipping business model and what you need to look out for before making a decision (Chapter 3)

- How to start your own dropshipping business including the potential business structure to consider, how to set up a company if you're living outside the US, how much you'll need to start and sources of funding (Chapter 4)
- How the supply chain and fulfilment process works – illustrated with an example transaction (Chapter 5)
- Analysis of 3 potential sales channel for your dropshipping business - including their respective pros and cons (Chapter 6)
- How to do niche research and select winning products – including the tools you need and where to get them (Chapter 7)
- How to find reliable suppliers and manufacturers. As well as 6 things you need to look out for in fake suppliers (Chapter 8)
- How to manage multiple suppliers and the inventory they hold for you (Chapter 9)
- How to deal with security and fraud issues (Chapter 10)
- What you need to do to minimize chargebacks i.e. refund rates (Chapter 11)
- How to price accordingly especially when your supplier offers international shipment (Chapter 12)
- 10 beginner mistakes and how to avoid them (Chapter 13)
- 7 powerful strategies you can leverage to scale up your dropshipping business (Chapter 14)
- 15 practical tips and lessons from successful dropshippers (Chapter 15)

And much, much more!

Finally, because this book is enrolled in Kindle Matchbook Program, the **kindle edition of this book will be available to you for free** when you purchase the paperback version from Amazon.com.

If you're ready to take charge of your financial future, grab your copy of this book today! Start taking control of your life by learning how to create a stream of passive income that'll take care of you and your loved ones.

Available In Kindle, Paperback and Audio

Dropshipping and Facebook Advertising: Discover How to Make Money Online and Create Passive Income Streams With Dropshipping and Social Media Marketing

This is a **2-in-1 book bundle** consisting of the below books and split into 2 parts. Amazon will make the kindle edition available to you for FREE when you purchase the print version of this bundle from Amazon.com - **saving you roughly 25%** from the price of the individual paperbacks.

- Dropshipping – Discover How to Make Money Online, Build Sustainable Streams of Passive Income and Gain Financial Freedom Using The Dropshipping E-Commerce Business Model (Part 1)
- Facebook Advertising – Learn How to Make $10,000+ Each Month with Facebook Marketing (Part 2)

Available In Kindle, Paperback and Audio

Get this bundle at a 35% discount from Amazon.com

Real Estate Investing For Beginners: Earn Passive Income With Reits, Tax Lien Certificates, Lease, Residential & Commercial Real Estate

In this book, Amazon bestselling author, Michael Ezeanaka, provides a step-by-step analysis of 10 Real Estate business models that have the potential to earn you passive income. A quick overview of each business is presented and their liquidity, scalability, potential return on investment, passivity and simplicity are explored.

In this book, you'll discover:

- How to make money with Real Estate Investment Trusts – including an analysis of the impact of the economy on the income from REITs (Chapter 1)
- A step-by-step description of how a Real Estate Investment Groups works and how to make money with this business model (Chapter 2)
- How to become a limited partner and why stakeholders can influence the running of a Real Estate Limited Partnership even though they have no direct ownership control in it (Chapter 3)
- How to protect yourself as a general partner (Chapter 3)
- Why tax lien certificates are one of the most secure investments you can make and how to diversify your portfolio of tax lien certificates (Chapter 4)
- Strategies you can employ to earn passive income from an empty land (Chapter 5)
- Two critical factors that are currently boosting the industrial real estate market and how you can take advantage of them (Chapter 6)
- Some of the most ideal locations to set up industrial real estate properties in the US, Asia and Europe (**Chapter 6**)
- Why going for long term leases (instead of short term ones) can significantly increase you return on investment from your industrial real estate properties (Chapter 6)
- Why commercial properties can serve as an excellent hedge against inflation – including two ways you can make money with commercial properties (Chapter 7)
- How long term leases and potential 'turnover rents' can earn you significant sums of money from Retail real estate properties and why they are very sensitive to the state of the economy (**Chapter 8**)
- More than 10 zoning rights you need to be aware of when considering investing in Mixed-Use properties (**Chapter 9**)
- 100 Tips for success that will help you minimize risks and maximize returns on your real estate investments

And much, much more!

PLUS, **BONUS MATERIALS**: you can download the author's Real Estate Business Scorecard which neatly summarizes, in alphabetical order, each business model's score across those 5 criteria i.e. liquidity, scalability, potential return on investment, passivity and simplicity!

Finally, because this book is enrolled in Kindle Matchbook Program, the **kindle edition of this book will be available to you for free** when you purchase the paperback version from Amazon.com.

If you're ready to take charge of your financial future, grab your copy of This Book today!

Available In Kindle, Paperback and Audio

Credit Card And Credit Repair Secrets: Discover How To Repair Your Credit, Get A 700+ Credit Score, Access Business Startup Funding, And Travel For Free Using Reward Cards

Are you sick and tired of paying huge interests on loans due to poor credit scores? Are you frustrated with not knowing where or how to get the necessary capital you need to start your business? Would you like to get all these as well as discover how you can travel the world for FREE?

If so, you'll love Credit Card and Credit Repair Secrets.

Imagine knowing simple do-it-yourself strategies you can employ to repair your credit profile, protect it from identity theft, access very cheap and affordable funding for your business and travel the world without any out of pocket expense!

This can be your reality. You can learn how to do all these and more. Moreover, you may be surprised by how simple doing so is.

In this book, you'll discover:

- **3 Types of consumer credit (And How You Can Access Them!)**
- How To Read, Review and Understand Your Credit Report (Including a Sample Letter You Can Send To Dispute Any Inaccuracy In It)
- **How To Achieve a 700+ Credit Score (And What To Do If You Have No FICO Score)**
- How To Monitor Your Credit Score (Including the difference between hard and soft inquiries)
- **What The VantageScore Model Is, It's Purpose, And How It Differs From The FICO Score Model**
- The Factors That Impact Your Credit Rating. Including The Ones That Certainly Don't - Despite What People Say!
- **Which Is More Important: Payment History Or Credit Utilization? (The Answer May Surprise You)**
- Why You Should Always Check Your Credit Report (At least Once A Month!)
- **How Credit Cards Work (From The Business And Consumer Perspective)**
- Factors You Need To Consider When Choosing A Credit Card (Including How To Avoid A Finance Charge on Your Credit Card)
- **How To Climb The Credit Card Ladder And Unlock Reward Points**
- Which Is More Appropriate: A Personal or Business Credit Card? (Find Out!)
- **How to Protect Your Credit Card From Identity Theft**
- Sources of Fund You Can Leverage To Grow Your Business

And much, much more!

An Identity Theft Resource Center (ITRC) report shows that 1,579 data breaches exposed about 179 million identity records in 2017. Being a victim of an identity scam can cause you a lot of problems. One of the worst cases would be the downfall of your credit score. You don't have to fall victim to it.

This book gives you a simple, but incredibly effective, step-by-step process you can use to build, protect and leverage your stellar credit profile to enjoy a financially stress-free life! It's practical. It's actionable. And if you follow it closely, it'll deliver extraordinary results!

PLUS BONUS - because this book is enrolled in Kindle Matchbook Program, the **kindle edition of this book will be available to you for free** when you purchase the paperback version from Amazon.com.

If you're ready to take charge of your financial future, grab your copy of This Book today!

Available In Kindle, Paperback and Audio

Real Estate Investing And Credit Repair: Discover How To Earn Passive Income With Real Estate, Repair Your Credit, Fund Your Business, And Travel For Free Using Reward Credit Cards

This is a **2-in-1 book bundle** consisting of the below books and split into 2 parts. Amazon will make the kindle edition available to you for FREE when you purchase the print version of this bundle from Amazon.com - **saving you roughly 25%** from the price of the individual paperbacks.

- Real Estate Investing For Beginners – Earn Passive Income With Reits, Tax Lien Certificates, Lease, Residential & Commercial Real Estate (Part 1)
- Credit Card And Credit Repair Secrets – Discover How To Repair Your Credit, Get A 700+ Credit Score, Access Business Startup Funding, And Travel For Free Using Reward Cards (Part 2)

Available In Kindle, Paperback and Audio

Get this bundle at a 35% discount from Amazon.com

Passive Income With Dividend Investing: Your Step-By-Step Guide To Make Money In The Stock Market Using Dividend Stocks

Have you always wanted to put your money to work in the stock market and earn passive income with dividend stocks?

What would you be able to achieve with a step-by-step guide designed to help you grow your money, navigate the dangers in the stock market and minimize the chance of losing your capital?

Imagine not having to rely solely on a salary or a pension to survive. Imagine having the time, money and freedom to pursue things you're passionate about, whether it's gardening, hiking, reading, restoring a classic car or simply spending time with your loved ones.

This book can help you can create this lifestyle for yourself and your loved ones!

Amazon bestselling author, Michael Ezeanaka, takes you through a proven system that'll help you to build and grow a sustainable stream of passive dividend income. He'll show you, step by step, how to identify stocks to purchase, do accurate due diligence, analyze the impact of the economy on your portfolio and when to consider selling.

In this book, you'll discover:

- Why investing in dividend stocks can position you to benefit tremendously from the "Baby Boomer Boost" (Chapter 1)
- **Which certain industry sectors tend to have a higher dividend payout ratio and why? (Chapter 2)**
- How to time your stock purchase around ex-dividend dates so as to take advantage of discounted share prices (Chapter 2)
- **Why a stock that is showing growth beyond its sustainable rate may indicate some red flags. (Chapter 2)**
- 5 critical questions you need to ask in order to assess if a company's debt volume will affect your dividend payment (Chapter 3)
- **How high dividend yield strategy can result in low capital gain taxes (Chapter 4)**
- Reasons why the average lifespan of a company included in the S&P 500 plummeted from 67 years in the 1920s to just 15 years in 2015. (Chapter 5)
- **A blueprint for selecting good dividend paying stocks (Chapter 6)**
- The vital information you need to look out for when reading company financial statements (Chapter 7)
- **A strategy you can use to remove the emotion from investing, as well as, build wealth cost efficiently (Chapter 8)**
- An affordable way to diversify your portfolio if you have limited funds (Chapter 9)
- **Why you may want to think carefully before selling cyclical stocks with high P/E ratio (Chapter 10)**

And much, much more!

PLUS BONUS - because this book is enrolled in Kindle Matchbook Program, the **kindle edition of this book will be available to you for free** when you purchase the paperback version from Amazon.com.

Whether you're a student, corporate executive, entrepreneur, or stay-at-home parent, the tactics described in this book can set the stage for a financial transformation.

If you're ready to build and grow a steady stream of passive dividend income, Grab your copy of this book today!

Available In Kindle, Paperback and Audio